The Music Producer's Guide To EQ

Published by Stereo Output Limited, company number 11174059

ISBN number 978-1-739996574

Copyright © Ashley Hewitt 2023

Ashley Hewitt has asserted his right under the Copyright, Designs and Patents Act 1988 to be identified as the author of this work.

All rights reserved. No part of this publication may be reproduced, stored in a retrieval system, or transmitted in any form or by any means, electronic, mechanical, photocopying, recording or otherwise, without the prior permission of the copyright holder except in the case of brief quotations embodied in critical views and certain other non-commercial uses permitted by copyright law.

The Music Producer's Guide is an independent series of books, and has not been authorised, sponsored, or otherwise approved by Ableton AG, MeldaProduction or any other company where screenshots of their products appear herein.

Please go to www.stereooutput.com to contact us or follow us on various social media channels.

Stereo Output

Contents

Introduction 1

Chapter 1: Filter Theory 2

Chapter 2: The Frequency Spectrum and the Harmonic Series 19

Chapter 3: How To EQ Individual Instruments 28

Chapter 4: Types of EQ 54

Chapter 5: How to Operate an EQ 60

Chapter 6: Practical EQ Tips 68

Chapter 7: Real EQ Use: Shaping 76

Chapter 8: Real EQ Use: Balancing 85

Chapter 9: Advanced EQ Techniques 101

Conclusion 112

Appendix: Exercise Answers 113

Introduction

EQ, or equalisation, is both one of the simplest and one of the most powerful effects in music production. It can shape the timbre of any element of your mix. It can help you blend elements of your mix, and it can help individual instruments stand out.

The simplicity of an EQ effects unit can deceive you into thinking that it's easy to use proficiently, whereas EQ can actually take a long time to master. Thankfully, there are certain underlying concepts and techniques that can help you gain a competent understanding of EQ use fairly quickly. In this book, we will be looking into some of them, such as:

- Filter theory
- The frequency range and harmonic series
- The frequency range of commonly used instruments
- Types of EQ
- Fundamental EQ techniques
- Practical EQ techniques to shape instruments
- Practical EQ techniques to balance two or more instruments
- Advanced EQ techniques

If you're new to EQing, or have struggled to use it, this book will help you. By the end, you should have gained the required skills to a very good level of proficiency and be able to apply EQ correctly in any music production situation you come across in your musical career.

However, practice makes perfect! Therefore, offered at the end of most Chapters, there will be exercises. Even if you've undertaken something like these exercises before, it is worth your completing them! It will help to improve your knowledge and understanding of

Chapter 1: Filter Theory

The premise underlying EQ is fairly straightforward. Sounds generate energy at various frequencies, and EQ allows us to increase or decrease the amplitude of sounds across the frequency spectrum. We might, for example, choose to increase the low frequency content of a sound whilst attenuating its high frequency content, or isolate the central frequency content of a sound only.

Whilst EQ may seem complex, it's constructed from a series of filters working together to create a unique shape.

Even a complex shape such as the one shown in Figure 1.1 below is just three filters put together:

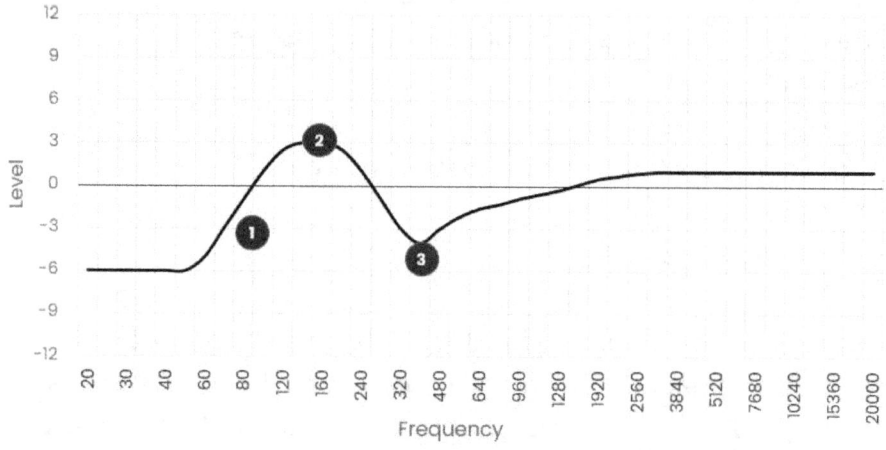

Figure 1.1: This EQ shape is composed of three filters.

If you are therefore going to construct your own EQ shapes, you need to begin by understanding the fundamental filter types from which all EQ is constructed.

Filters are not merely a music production device; we can find them everywhere. Your broadband equipment uses filters to block out unwanted noise on the phone line. Your speakers use filters to decide which audio signals to send to the different speaker cones. Your analogue radio uses filters - when you tune it, you're merely filtering out all the frequencies you want it to exclude.

In music, filters are used to shape sounds – for example, attenuating the high elements of a synthesizer patch, or adjusting the bass of a pad.

In EQ, there are four primary filter types:

• Pass filters: low-pass and high-pass;

• Shelf filters: low-shelf and high-shelf;

• Bell;

• Notch.

You may be familiar with, at minimum, low-pass and high-pass filters, particularly if you've programmed a synthesizer previously. If not, no problem! In this section we will explore each of these in more detail.

Low-pass and high-pass

Low-pass and high-pass are two of the most fundamental filter types, and you will use them a great deal.

In the context of low-pass and high-pass filters, to **pass** means *to allow a frequency band through the filter*. So, a low-pass filter allows low frequencies through, and a high-pass filter allows high frequencies through.

How do we define which frequencies are low, and which are high? A parameter called the **cutoff** defines this. The cutoff is roughly the point in the frequency spectrum at which the filter starts working. So, on a low-pass filter, frequencies *below* the cutoff will be allowed through. On a high-pass filter, frequencies *above* the cutoff will be allowed through.

However, filters don't work abruptly. If the cutoff of a low-pass filter is set to 1kHz, some frequencies above 1kHz will be allowed through. This is to do with how the analogue circuitry of filters work, but even in the computer era it sounds far more musical to have a gradual change in amplitude around the cutoff than an abrupt one. A parameter called the **roll-off** defines this steepness. A low roll-off is gentle, whereas a high roll-off is steep.

An illustration of a low-pass filter on a frequency spectrum, with its cutoff and roll-off, is shown below, in Figure 1.2. As you can see, a 12dB roll-off means that frequencies are filtered out gently, whereas a 48dB roll-off means that frequencies are filtered out sharply.

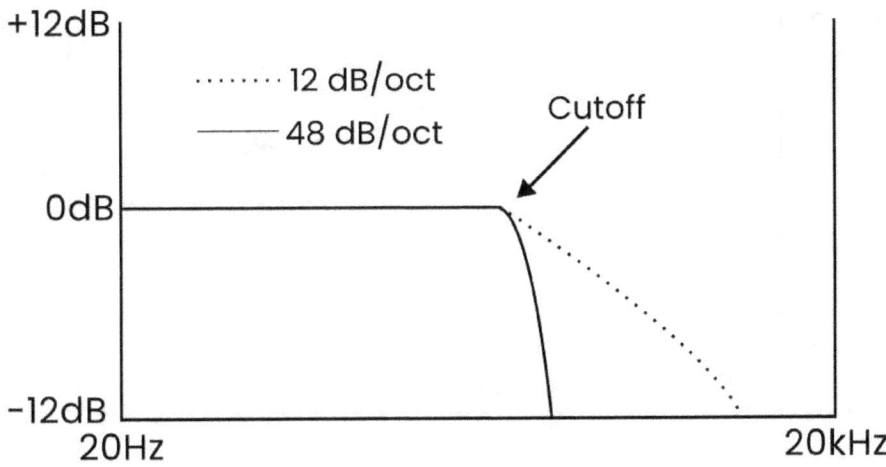

Figure 1.2: An illustration of a low-pass filter.

You can see the area where the filtering starts, and you can see two different roll-off settings. At 48 dB/oct, frequencies above the cutoff are attenuated sharply, whereas at 12dB/oct, frequencies above the cutoff are attenuated more gently. The 12dB/oct roll-off will make for a gentler, more natural sound – but at the expense of accuracy, because this will still let a lot of content through above the cutoff.

An illustration of a high-pass filter is in Figure 1.3. Notice how it's pretty much a mirror image of the low-pass filter. This is because the functionality of low-pass filters and high-pass filters is similar – the difference is whether it's frequencies above or below the cutoff that are allowed through.

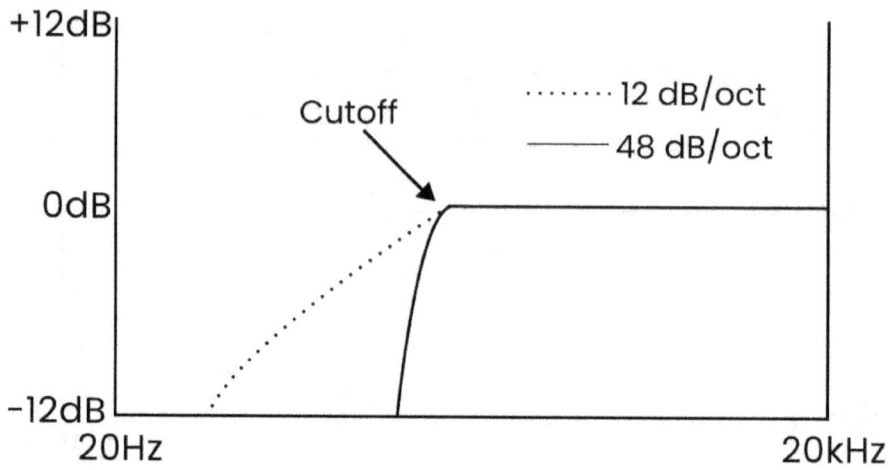

Figure 1.3: *An illustration of a high-pass filter.*

Low-pass and high-pass filters are commonly used in EQ to eliminate frequencies, for example removing most of the boomy bottom end of a bass guitar or getting rid of some harsh top-end in a drum recording. Sometimes, however, rather than elimination, you may want gentle attenuation or increase of the top or bottom end of an instrument. This is where low-shelf and high-shelf filters come in.

Low-shelf and high-shelf

Shelving filters are low-pass and high-pass's gentler cousins. Rather than eliminate a frequency range, they let you increase or decrease the amplitude of sounds above or below the selected frequency.

A low-shelf filter lets you boost or attenuate lower frequencies, leaving higher frequencies untouched, and a high-shelf filter lets you boost or attenuate higher frequencies, leaving lower frequencies untouched.

There are three components to shelving filters:

• The gain, which is the extent to which the affected frequency is boosted or attenuated.

• The slope, which controls the size of the *transition band*, which is the area that transitions from untouched to boosting or attenuating.

• The frequency, which defines whereabouts the transition will occur.

I illustrate these three components in Figure 1.4, which shows a low shelf filter:

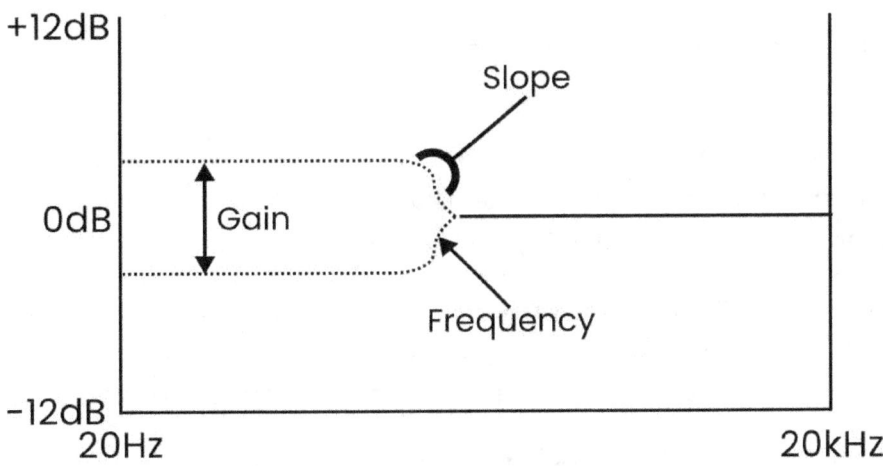

Figure 1.4: *An illustration of a low-shelf filter.*

As you can see, there are three stages: the unaffected area, the affected area below the selected frequency, and the transition band between the two.

In a low-shelf filter, all sounds below the selected frequency are increased or decreased in volume. This is unlike the low-pass and high-pass filters that work using a curve: in shelving filters, everything past the slope is horizontal. This means that the same change in amplitude applies to all affected frequencies below the slope.

Whereas the frequency in low-pass and high-pass filters is fairly well defined, there are three different ways to define the point at which the shelving filter transitions from the inactive area to the active area:

• The cut-off, which is the point at which 3dB of gain change occurs.

• The centre frequency, which is the mid-point of the *transition band*, that area between the untouched frequency and the boosted or attenuated frequency.

• The corner frequency, which is where the full amount of gain change is reached.

Thankfully, the interface of EQ plugins will give you enough visual information to make correct decisions without having to know precisely how the frequency parameter was calculated.

Shelving filters are mostly used when a broad, gentle boost or cut is required to a frequency range at the ends of a frequency spectrum. For example, to highlight the high frequencies of a pad.

An example of a high-shelf filter is shown in Figure 1.5:

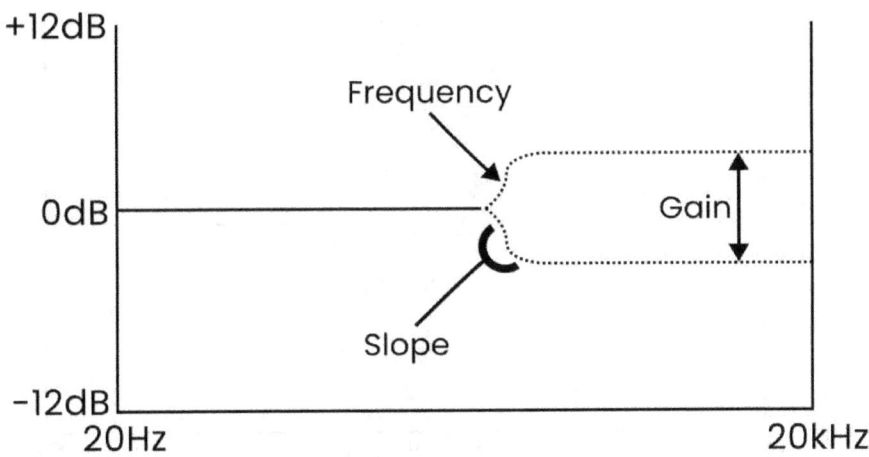

Figure 1.5: An illustration of a high-shelf filter.

As shown, a high-shelf filter is a mirror image of a low-shelf filter, with the area above the selected frequency being affected. Just like in low or high-pass filters, the difference between low and high-shelf filters is whether it's the frequencies above or below the selected *frequency* that are affected.

Bell filter

A bell filter allows you to boost or attenuate a specific frequency range in isolation. It's most commonly used towards the centre of the frequency range. For example, if a synthesizer patch had an unpleasant resonance at 4kHz, you could attenuate it, whilst leaving lower and higher frequencies unaltered. I illustrated a bell filter in Figure 1.6:

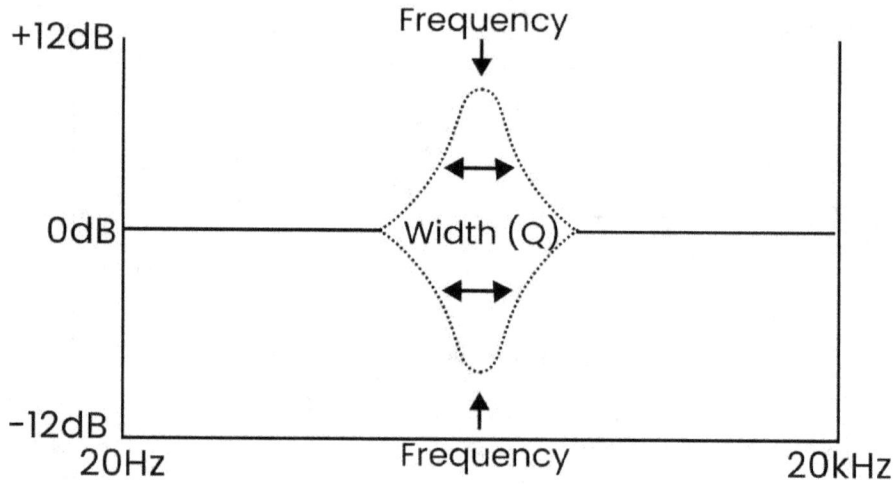

Figure 1.6: An illustration of a bell filter.

As you can see, this filter can be moved anywhere in the frequency range and can boost or attenuate the selected frequency to any extent.

Remember, however, that filters do not work in isolation. You couldn't, for example, cut 1kHz, but leave 999Hz untouched. This is where the term bell comes into play, because to either side of your selected frequency, there will be an area where it transitions to the rest of the EQ. This leads to a shape like the bell curve seen in statistics. The width (and therefore sharpness) of the curve can be controlled using a parameter called Q, but we'll look at that in more detail later in this Chapter.

The bell filter is the one most frequently used in EQ, because it allows for precision when boosting or attenuating a frequency.

Notch

A notch filter, also known as a band-stop filter, allows you to eliminate a specific frequency, as shown in Figure 1.7:

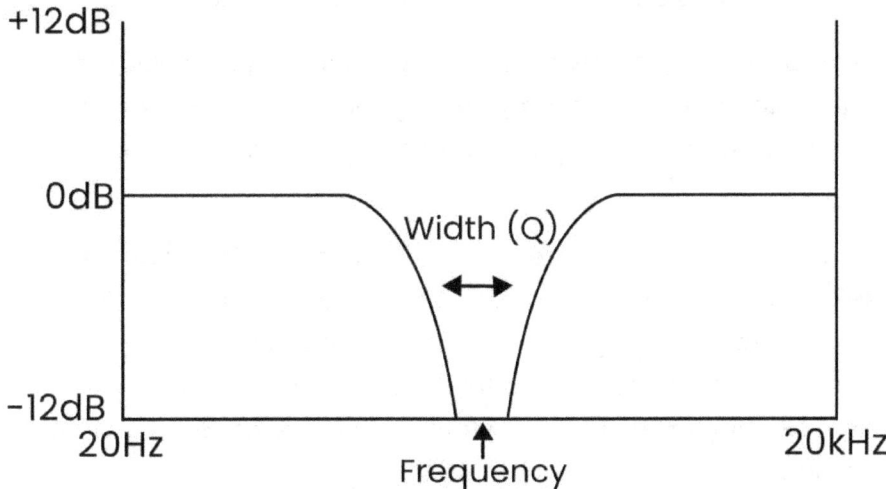

Figure 1.7: An illustration of a notch filter.

The key difference between a notch filter and a bell filter is that the attenuation of a notch filter is severe, effectively removing the selected frequency altogether. Consider it like a low-pass and a high-pass filter put together, controlled by a single frequency.

The width of the attenuation around the chosen frequency - and therefore the sharpness of the transition in and out of the selected frequency - can be chosen. In EQ, we achieved this using the Q function.

The notch filter is one of the lesser-used filters in music production – eliminating a central frequency can have a drastic effect on the timbre of your sound!

Q

All four of the primary filter types we've just looked at in this section have one key parameter that unites them: Q. Short for Quality Factor, Q defines just how selective your filter is.

A high Q means the filter acts more strongly on your selected frequencies, and less strongly on neighbouring frequencies. You may assume that if Q defines quality, you always want the highest possible Q.

However, in music, producers may find that a lower Q can be useful. Rather than generating a loss of precision, a lower Q means gentler filtering of the audio around the selected frequency, leading to instruments retaining more of their natural timbre. Plugin developers therefore let the user choose how much Q to apply.

As an example, Figure 1.8 shows two low-pass filters, one with low Q, and the other with high Q:

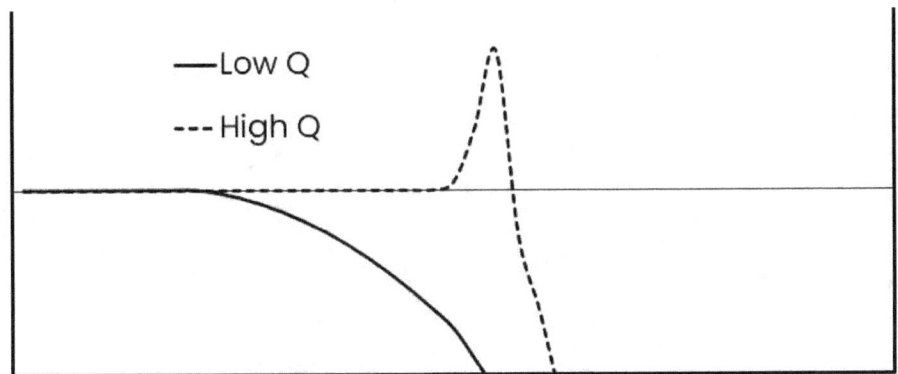

Figure 1.8: A comparison of low Q and high Q on a low-pass filter. A high-pass filter would show the same effect, albeit flipped horizontally.

As you can see, a low Q means that there is a slow roll-off of frequencies around the cut-off point. This creates a gentle smoothing of frequencies.

On the other hand, a high Q means that whilst there is a fast roll-off of frequencies around the cut-off, this creates a sharp resonant peak around the cut-off. You may be familiar with this peak from programming synthesizer filters, where it is an adjustable parameter called Resonance.

This means that when increasing Q on low or high-pass filters, you're trading precision for smoothness.

In shelving filters, a low Q creates a gradual change in amplitude across frequency, making for a smooth curve that may lack some accuracy. A high Q, however, will generate a resonant trough on one side of the central frequency, and a resonant peak on the other - almost creating an S shape. I illustrate these in Figure 1.9:

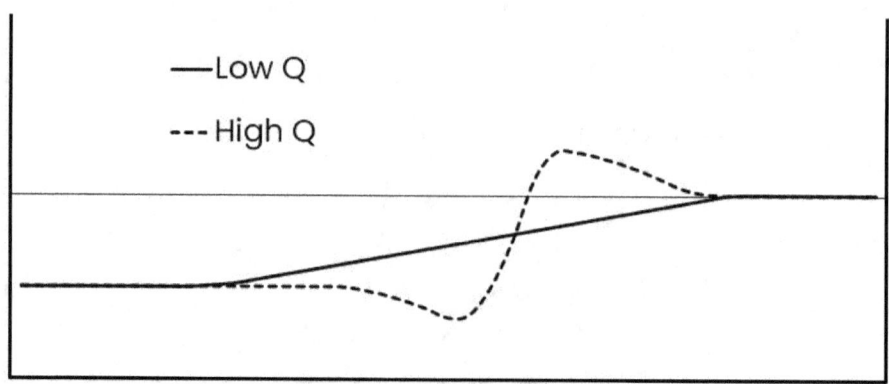

Figure 1.9: A comparison of low and high Q on a low-shelf filter. A high-shelf filter would show the same effect, albeit flipped horizontally.

You can see that this means that paradoxically, you may achieve *better* precision and control with a low Q when using shelving filters. Of course, when adjusting Q for yourself, you will find a compromise that balances precision with filter shape.

With bell filters, a low Q creates a broad peak that encompasses most of the frequency range. A high Q on bell filters generates an accurate peak, which, unlike the resonant peaks and troughs of pass and shelving filters, doesn't contain any significant artefacts. This is shown in Figure 1.10:

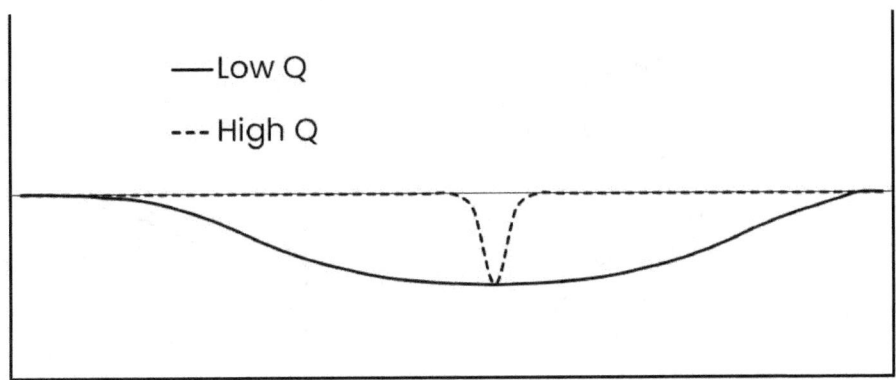

Figure 1.10: A comparison of low Q and high Q on a bell filter.

Unlike pass and shelving filters, a high Q doesn't cause any significant downstream problems such as major resonances on bell filters. Therefore, the application of Q is a question of which timbre you want.

Finally, let's look at notch filters in Figure 1.11. As you can see, a low Q creates a wide gap, with gentle curves that occupy a significant amount of the frequency range. A high Q on notch filters makes for an exceptionally precise notch filter, which - as on bell filters - doesn't contain any artefacts or resonant peaks.

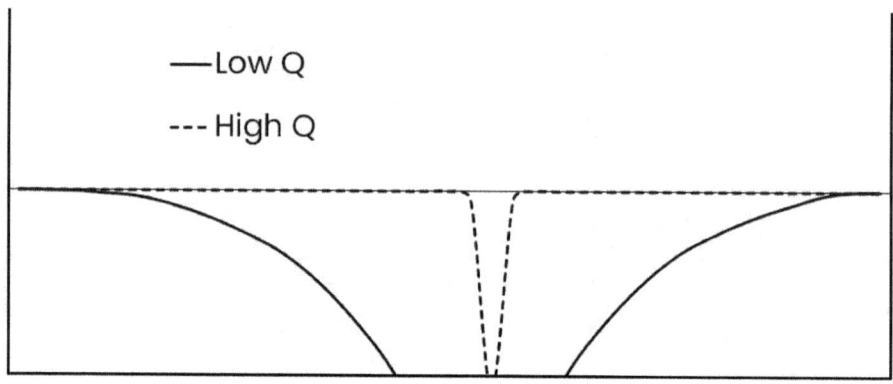

Figure 1.11: A comparison of low Q and high Q on a notch filter.

Let's summarise what we've discussed so far:

- Low-pass, high-pass, and notch filters are used to eliminate high, low, and middling frequencies, respectively.
- Roll-off defines the steepness of the filter curve on low-pass and high-pass filters.
- The slope defines the area of the 'transition band' between the affected area and unaffected area on shelving filters.
- Shelving filters are used to boost or cut a range at either end of the frequency spectrum.
- Bell filters are used to make precise changes at any point in the frequency spectrum.
- Q is an important parameter that governs a filter's accuracy, but too high a Q can generate unpleasant resonant peaks on low-pass, high-pass, and shelving filters.

Table 1.1 is a table summarising the six filter types we've covered in this Chapter:

Table 1.1: A summary of all filter types discussed in this Chapter.

Filter type	Effect	Shape
Low-pass	Eliminates frequencies above the threshold.	
High-pass	Eliminates frequencies below the threshold.	
Low-shelf	Attenuates or boosts all frequencies below the threshold.	
High-shelf	Attenuates or boosts all frequencies above the threshold.	
Notch	Eliminates frequencies at, and either side of the threshold.	
Bell	Attenuates or boosts frequencies at, and either side of the threshold.	

Through these six filters you can create any conceivable shape, providing you with near limitless options for shaping the timbre of your sound.

Here's a quick quiz, to test your knowledge so far.

Exercises

Answer these questions. If you get stuck, the answers are in the Appendix at the back of this book.

1. If you wanted to eliminate frequencies under a set threshold, which filter would you choose?
2. If you wanted to add a gentle boost to a frequency in the middle of the frequency range, which filter would you choose?
3. If you wanted to attenuate all frequencies above a set threshold, which filter would you choose?
4. If your EQing required precision, would you use low Q or high Q?
5. What is "roll-off"?

The next step is to understand the qualities of the frequency spectrum as we hear it in music.

Chapter 2: The Frequency Spectrum and the Harmonic Series

Now that we know that EQ is a series of filters, we need to know *what* to filter. Therefore, let's look at two fundamental topics: the frequency spectrum, and the harmonic series.

The Frequency Spectrum

Humans can generally hear sound between 20Hz and 20kHz, although our ability to hear the very upper end of that spectrum degrades as we age.

If we wish to understand this spectrum in a way that's applicable to music production, it helps to simplify it. To do this, we can break the frequency spectrum down into fixed 'bands'. Because the frequency spectrum is a linear range, there are many ways that people do this.

As a starting point, however, I like to break the frequency range down into six bands, as shown in Figure 2.1:

Sub bass	Bass	Low Mids	Mids	Upper Mids	Highs
20Hz–80Hz	80Hz–225Hz	225Hz–500Hz	500Hz–2.5kHz	2.5kHz–7kHz	7kHz–20kHz

20Hz … 20kHz

Figure 2.1: A breakdown of the frequency range into six areas.

Each of these six areas corresponds to a section of the frequency range that has its own qualities, and its own implications for your mix.

Remember, when working with these bands, that there's some flexibility and subjectivity. If you have an instrument that occasionally delves from one band into another, that's not a problem. Using these bands is merely a mental tool to help you understand the frequency range, and its effects on your mix and listener. Consider also that many instruments occupy several of these bands – but we'll look more at that later.

Let's begin by looking at the lowest frequency band – sub bass.

Sub bass (20Hz-80Hz)

Sub bass is the very bottom of the frequency range. It creates *rumble*, *weight* and *intensity*. It is the frequency range that vibrates your ribcage on a big club sound system.

Despite its power, it is not audible on smaller speaker systems, such as your radio alarm clock, because reproducing these frequencies requires either big speaker cones, or clever technical tricks.

It is best to work on this range in the studio using good-quality audio equipment, such as excellent monitor speakers (e.g., Yamaha HS8), or, at a push, open-back headphones. Check your equipment's user manual to find out the lowest frequency ranges that it can reproduce. Very few speaker systems can reproduce anything below 30Hz.

If you're working in acoustic music, you will encounter this frequency range during periods of emphasis, for example an emphasised kick drum. However, electronic music is where this frequency is almost constantly at a high intensity.

If you are writing electronic music, this frequency range will establish the foundation of the whole track, as this is where important elements of your kick drum and sub bass will reside.

We'll look in more depth at getting this area right later in the book. First, however, we'll look in more depth at another important frequency range: the bass.

Bass (80Hz-225Hz)

Bass gives a track *boom*, *punch* and *energy*. Bass guitars, kick drums, and many synthesized basslines occupy this frequency range.

The bass range needs careful balance against the ranges on either side of it. Many instruments that occupy the sub-bass frequency range also occupy the bass frequency range. On the other side, many instruments that occupy the low mids, such as pads, or leads, can also occupy the bass range.

This need for balance means that you, as a producer, must be selective about which elements you allow to occupy the bass range – and which you don't.

Because it is the frequency range that gives your track *punch* and energy, you want your *punchiest*, most *energetic* instruments to be heard here.

Let's explore the next frequency range upwards – low mids.

Low Mid (225Hz-500Hz)

The low mid area creates *depth* and *body*, but also *mud*.

The low mid area marks the transition from the bass frequencies to the melodic instruments (such as vocals, pads, or stabs). It contains both the harmonics from your bass instruments, such as your kick and bass, as well as the lower end of your melodic instruments, and your percussive instruments like clap and snare.

Whereas the bass and sub bass carry a lot of energy, the low mid can be a more lethargic area. It gives your instruments definition, but this frequency range can get crowded. The right amount of low mids is crucial to your mix. Too much presence in the low mid area leads to a *muddy*, cluttered mix. Too little presence in the low mid area leads to a hollow sounding track. The right amount, however, gives your track warmth and fullness.

Mid (500Hz-2.5kHz)

The mid area contains *musicality*, *punch*, and *presence*. This is where the higher end of your melodic instruments lives. The focus points of your track (e.g., your leads, vocals and pads) should have lots of space in this range. Cutting the mids of melodic instruments can make them sound hollow and cheap. The lower end of this area can contribute to instruments, particularly drums, sounding boxy, like cardboard being struck.

This is a delicate area to get right but making sure you choose which instruments receive priority can help improve any balancing issues you may have.

Upper Mid (2.5kHz-7kHz)

This area is where *crunch*, *sibilance* and *clarity* are found. The top end of your snares, hi-hats and claps occupies this space. Too little of this frequency range, and your mix will sound dull, lacking in presence. Too much, however, particularly around 2kHz-5kHz, and your mix will sound aggressive, grating, brittle and fatiguing, like nails on a chalkboard.

Given that this area is so important to your percussive instruments, you can achieve a lot of balance by dealing with any resonances that may appear from your percussive instruments, to ensure that these instruments have clarity, but don't become grating. We'll look at how to do this later in the book.

High (7kHz-20kHz)

The high area is the absolute top end of the frequency spectrum. It gives your mix *sparkle*, *air* and *brightness*. It's a suitable area to focus on when working with high-frequency percussion.

Elements that occupy this frequency range only can sound like they float above the mix, which is why producers often add instruments like ride cymbals, shakers, or tambourines to their mix.

However, let's be clear - very few sounds occupy a single part of the frequency spectrum. This is because of the vital presence of harmonics, which we'll look at next.

Before we look at harmonics, let's summarise what we've learned about the frequency spectrum so far:

Table 2.1: A summary of the frequency range.

Frequency range	Frequency	Qualities	Things to look out for
20Hz–80Hz	Sub bass	Rumble, weight, intensity.	
80Hz–225Hz	Bass	Boom, punch, energy.	
225Hz–500Hz	Low mid	Depth, body.	Too much of this range can lead to mud.
500Hz–2.5kHz	Mid	Musicality, punch, presence.	Too little of this range can lead to boxiness.
2.5kHz–7kHz	Upper mid	Crunch, sibilance, clarity.	Too much of this range can be grating.
7kHz–20kHz	High	Sparkle, air, brightness.	

Harmonics

The harmonic series is the phenomenon that underpins all music.

When someone plays a musical instrument, such as a piano, or guitar, this creates a vibration at the frequency of the note played – the fundamental frequency. Besides this vibration, there is also a vibration at double its frequency, triple its frequency, four times its frequency, and so on – at a lesser volume to the fundamental frequency. These additional notes are called the harmonic series, and the frequencies generated are called harmonic overtones, often shortened to *harmonics*. They are illustrated in Figure 3.2, using MeldaProduction's MAnalyzer:

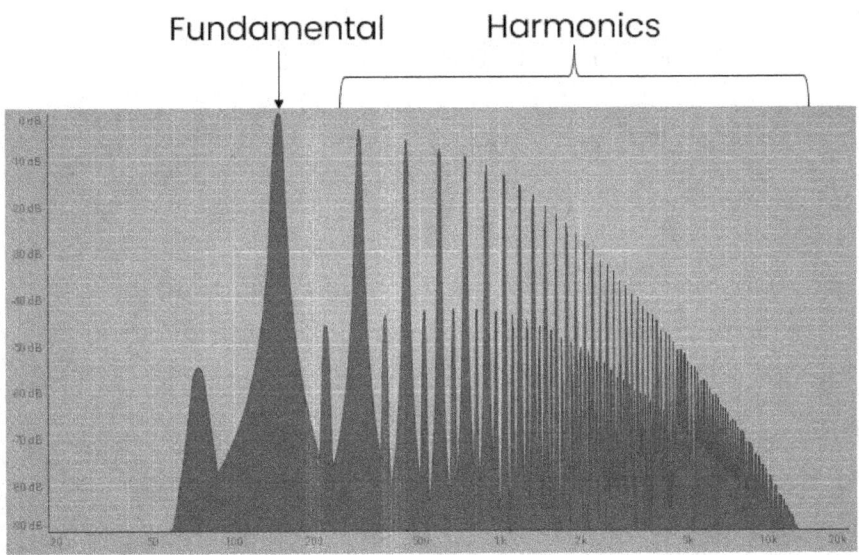

Figure 1.4: The harmonic series.

For example, if a guitar string is played at 440Hz, it will generate harmonics. Table 2.2 shows the first seven:

Table 2.2: The first seven harmonics of 440Hz.

Harmonic	Pitch	Nearest musical note
Fundamental	440Hz	A4
2nd harmonic	880Hz	A5
3rd harmonic	1320Hz	E6
4th harmonic	1760Hz	A6
5th harmonic	2200Hz	C#
6th harmonic	2640Hz	E7
7th harmonic	3080Hz	G7

Each of these harmonics is usually a lower amplitude than the harmonic below it, although the extent to which they are lower depends on the instrument played.

Our ears cannot pick out these individual harmonics; we hear each note as the fundamental frequency. The harmonics, however, add colour and timbre to the tone. Each musical instrument creates a different balance of harmonics, which helps us distinguish one instrument from another.

It is important to bear these harmonics in mind when using EQ. When we look at the frequency analysis of a sound, we will see its fundamental and its harmonics. Most of the time, the fundamental is the leftmost, strongest frequency. The quieter peaks, cascading away to the right (as the frequency increases), are the harmonics.

We can change the timbre of a synthetic instrument by adjusting the relationship between the fundamental and the harmonics. However, if the fundamental is too quiet, the instrument can sound hollow or inauthentic. In the mixing process, overbearing harmonics can often be attenuated without having too much of an impact on the perception of the instrument.

Now that we've taken a broad look at the frequency spectrum, let's explore individual instruments in more depth, looking at how each of these interacts with the frequency spectrum within which they reside.

Exercises

Answer these questions. If you get stuck, the answers are in the Appendix at the back of this book.

1. Where on the frequency spectrum is the sub bass range?
2. What is a fundamental frequency?
3. What frequency is the third harmonic of a note playing at 800Hz?
4. In which part of the frequency spectrum would you find *sparkle*?

Chapter 3: How To EQ Individual Instruments

With our broad understanding of the frequency spectrum and harmonics, we can now look at individual instruments. Each instrument is different and requires treating differently. My aim with this chapter is to save you from hundreds of hours spent making basic mistakes. I hope that by the end, you'll know what to do (and what not to do) when EQing some of the most common instruments.

The prospect of looking at an instrument's presence across the entire frequency spectrum can be an intimidating one. After all, how do we know which part of the frequency spectrum affects an instrument's timbre?

Thankfully, producers can target specific areas of the frequency spectrum in each instrument to achieve their desired outcome. In music production circles, you'll hear these areas being referred to in descriptive, abstract terms, such as *sparkle*, *thud*, or *presence*, just like I used to describe the six areas of the frequency spectrum in Chapter 2.

In this Chapter, I shall reveal these frequency profiles for eleven common instruments. These will help you, in the long term, know where to start when looking to create your EQ curves. I summarise each instrument with a chart for easy reference.

When using EQ, you will often use spectrum analysis, a technique that provides a moving visualisation of the amplitude of each frequency. You can see a spectrum analysis for yourself by playing audio through a parametric EQ plugin in many DAWs, such as EQ Eight in Ableton Live, or Channel EQ in Logic Pro X.

These use an algorithm called Fast Fourier Transform, which transforms the sound of your instrument into a readable graph.

These visualisations are quite intuitive once you get used to them. The x-axis represents the frequency (from left to right), and the y-axis represents the amplitude (from bottom to top). As shown in Figure 3.1, a representation of the amplitude at each frequency is provided.

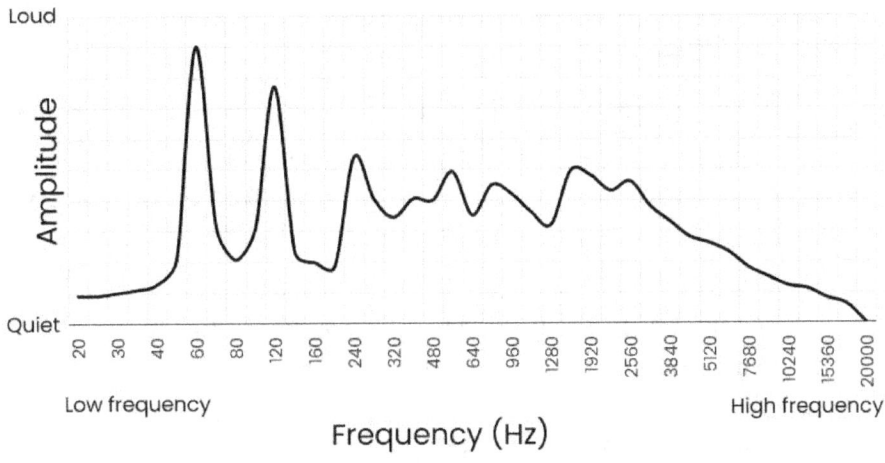

Figure 3.1: An example FFT analysis.

In this Chapter, we will look at the profile and example FFT representations of common instruments, so that you can see where the peaks and troughs are in the frequency range, and identify which frequencies may need adjusting when you use these instruments in your own work.

It's worth mentioning that these representations are based on averages of a few of the same instrument and won't be the exact frequency profile of the instruments that you use. However, they will provide you with a good starting point to understanding how these instruments occupy the frequency range – and what, therefore, to look out for.

Let's begin by looking at kickdrums.

Electronic kickdrums

808 and 909 kickdrums are the most prevalent kickdrums in recorded music. When tuned to the same pitch, they both have a similar frequency profile.

Areas to look out for

1. The first area to look at when EQing electronic kickdrums is the extremely low frequencies, usually under 40Hz. This *rumble* adds very little to your mix but takes up headroom in your mix - so it can be attenuated significantly.

2. The most important area is the sub-bass area between 40Hz and 80Hz. This provides much of your kick's overall *power*, but can take up a great deal of headroom, so be careful if you also have a sub bass present in this area.

3. 808 and 909 kicks have a significant *thump* around 100-220Hz. This is one of the most useful areas to manipulate if you're trying to blend your kick with your bass. Increasing the amplitude of this area makes your kick sound more prominent in the mix, allowing you to bring down the sub-bass area slightly to give your bass and sub-bass instruments more breathing space.

4. Whereas the 909 kickdrum rolls off quickly from 240Hz onwards, the 808's kick rolls off slowly. This area above 240Hz is full of rich harmonics on the 808. Those looking to emphasise their 808 kicks, particularly those writing trap music, may wish to increase the amplitude of this area -

just make sure that the kick is tuned to the same frequency as the bass. You can do this using a plugin containing a spectrum analyser to find out what frequency your fundamental is playing at. In the example shown below in Figure 3.2, MeldaProduction's MAnalyzer highlights G#1 as the fundamental:

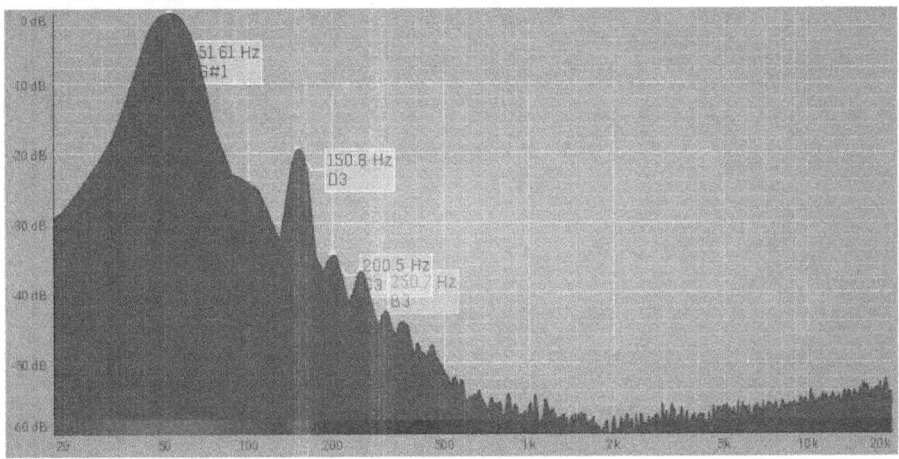

Figure 3.2: An 808 kick analysed using MeldaProduction's MAnalyzer.

5. Whereas the 808 kick's higher end is full of rich harmonics, the 909's higher end has more of a *click* sound. You can increase or decrease this *click* to affect the listener's perception of the presence of the kick. This is important in genres like Techno, where you may wish to increase this *click* in big room tracks but attenuate it in calmer sub-genres like Dub Techno. However, it does lack the warm, harmonic richness of the 808 kickdrum.

The estimated frequency profile of the 808 and 909 kickdrums is shown in Figure 3.3:

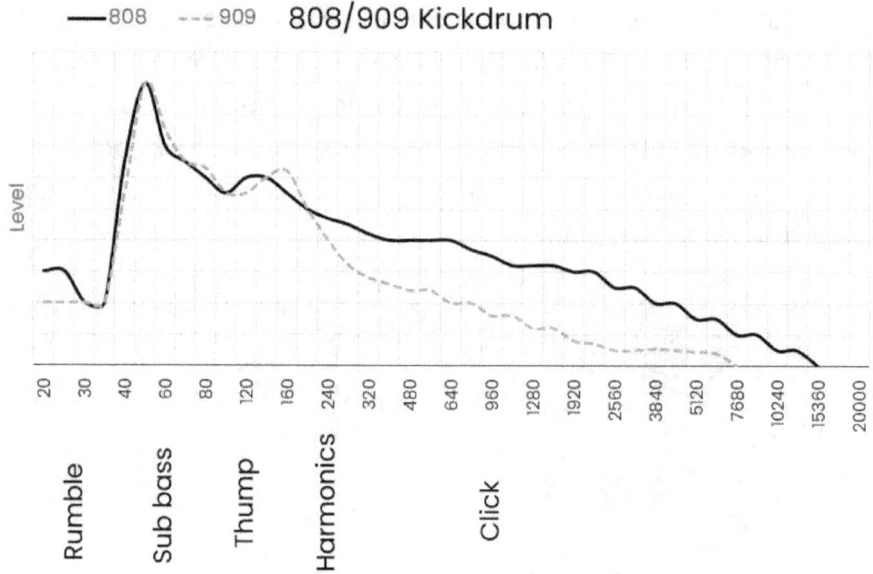

Figure 3.3: *The estimated frequency profile of an 808 and 909 kickdrum.*

Acoustic kickdrum

Acoustic kickdrums have a looser sound compared to the tight 808 and 909 kicks, because of the organic process of striking them.

<u>Areas to look out for</u>

1. Acoustic kickdrums have a wider area in the sub-bass frequency range. You can still find a rumble under 40Hz that can be removed, a sub bass around 40-80Hz, and a defined thump around 100-150Hz. The sub bass is less important to the sonic identity of an acoustic kick than it is to an electronic kick.

2. There is also more presence in the 200-1kHz area than in an electronic kickdrum. You can harness this to emphasise the kickdrum without creating too much conflict with your lower bass frequencies.

3. The *click* between 1kHz and 5kHz adds a lot to the definition of the acoustic kickdrum. In tracks where the kickdrum is front and centre of the listener's attention, this *click* is vital to give the kick clarity. You can increase this *click*'s amplitude if you wish to emphasise the kickdrum in your mix without increasing its bass presence.

You can see the estimated frequency profile of acoustic kickdrums in Figure 3.4:

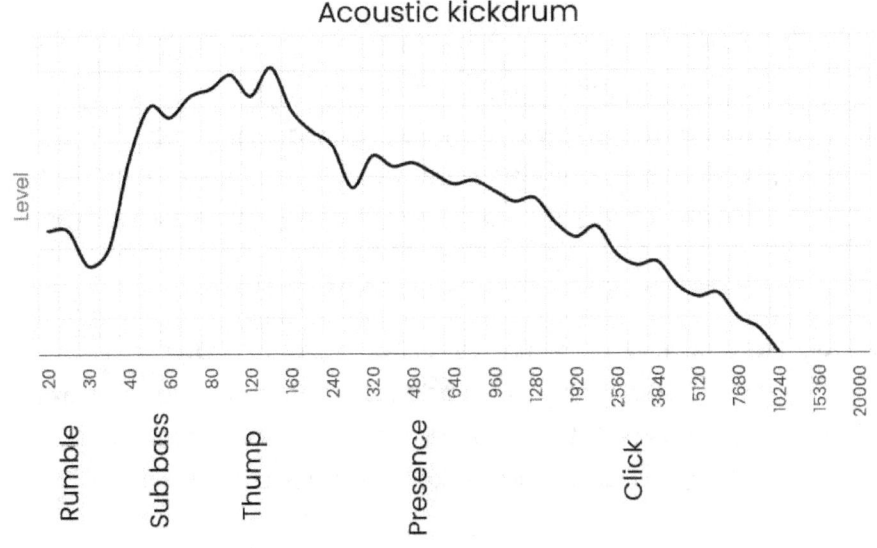

Figure 3.4: The estimated frequency profile of an acoustic kickdrum.

Next, let's look at some typical basses.

Harsh synth bass

You can find harsh synth basses in more aggressive electronic music subgenres, such as EDM, Dubstep, or drum and bass. They are characterised by a great deal of mid content.

<u>Areas to look out for</u>

1. The first section to look when EQing a harsh bass is the sub bass, usually under 80Hz. Some patches have a lot of sub bass present, others have little or none. Many producers choose to pair harsh basses with a separate sub bass track to have full control over both. If you do this, eliminate the sub bass area of your harsh bass using a high-pass filter, so that it doesn't conflict with your main sub bass.

2. The next area to look at is 80-300Hz. This is where a lot of warm harmonics live. You may wish to increase the amplitude of this *warmth*. Just be wary of conflicts with your kick. You can cut in this area if you feel your mix is too *muddy*, but make sure you don't detract too much from the bass's *warmth*.

3. Harsh basses often have a great deal of *growl*, found around 300Hz-1kHz. This adds a lot of energy to the mix but competes with the lower end of your lead instruments. Cutting this area can make your bass sound thin.

4. *Presence* is found around 2kHz-8kHz. You should boost this area if your bass is the focal point of your whole track, but you could cut it if you're writing in a more subdued style, such as minimal drum and bass.

5. Finally, harsh basses often contain *sparkle* above 8kHz. This can draw the listener's attention to your bass slightly, but it will compete with your higher percussion, such as your hi-hats and shakers.

A summary of the frequency profile of harsh synth basses is shown in Figure 3.5:

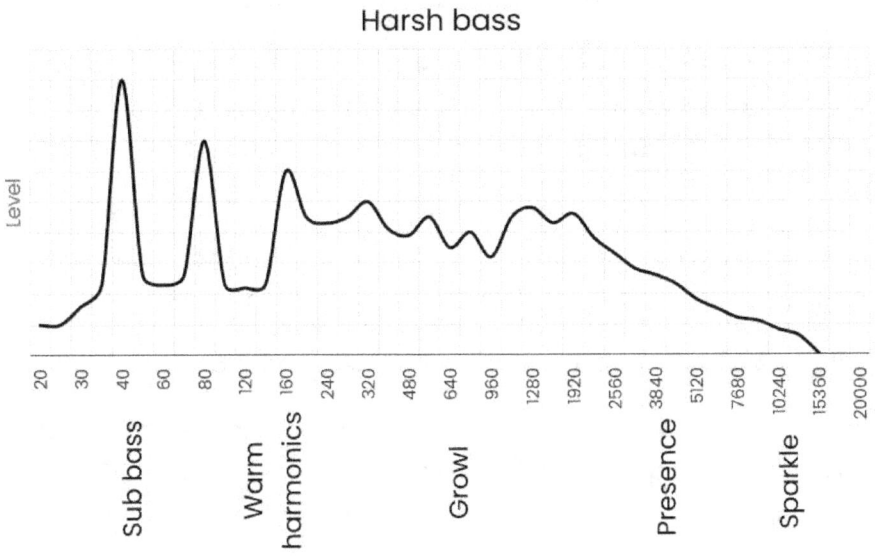

Figure 3.5: The estimated frequency profile of a harsh bass.

Synth sub bass

Synth sub basses can be found everywhere in electronic music. Because they're not audible on smaller speaker systems, they are more prevalent in music designed for club systems. In genres like drum and bass, producers sometimes combine them with a harsh bass to enhance control over the sub bass frequency - a clear instance of this can be heard in the track Stigma by Noisia.

However, in genres like Techno or Tech House, sub basses sometimes sit underneath the kickdrum, without an obvious bassline on top. An example of this can be heard in *Parallax View* by Benjamin Damage.

Synth sub basses often have far less harmonic content than their harsher siblings. How much harmonic content depends on the waveforms selected in the synthesizer's oscillators.

Sub basses are usually designed for sheer sonic power, and for that reason, they commonly use less harmonically rich waveforms, often using only one oscillator on a synthesizer.

A sine wave is the simplest of all waveforms because it contains no harmonics. This makes EQing unnecessary, as adjusting the amplitude of the signal performs the same function.

Triangle and square basses, however, generate harmonics.

When the note played is low enough to be considered a sub bass, there are two frequency bands to concern yourself with. EQing becomes about shaping the balance between the two bands.

Areas to look out for

1. The first area is the sub bass range, usually below 80Hz. This is where the fundamental frequency usually resides.

2. The second is the harmonics above 80Hz. These add presence, warmth and clarity to the sub bass. They are also in the frequency range of smaller speaker sets, such as Bluetooth speakers. If your track's only bass instrument is a sub bass, consider increasing the amplitude of these harmonics. You can even create new harmonics using a distortion plugin, particularly a valve emulation plugin that adds warm, even harmonics. However, if your sub bass is

paired with a harsher bass, you may not need these harmonics. In this case, reduce their amplitude to prevent conflict with your harsher bass.

The estimated frequency profile of two synthesizer sub bass waveforms can be seen in Figure 3.6:

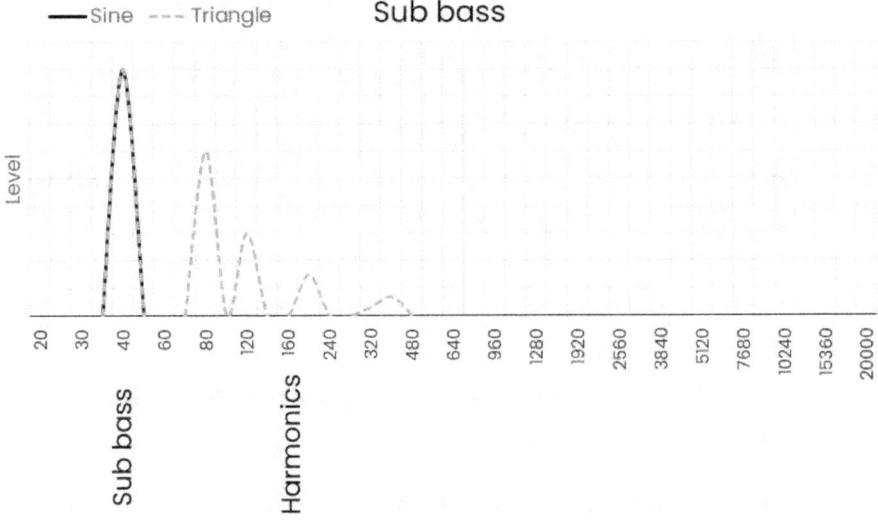

Figure 3.6: The estimated frequency profile of two sub basses: a sine wave, and a triangle wave.

Bass guitar

As organic, recorded instruments, bass guitars give the producer slightly less control than synth basses. Despite this, the principles of EQing a bass guitar remain similar to those of EQing a synth bass. The main thing to look out for is how much presence you wish to give the guitar in the mix.

Areas to look out for

1. The lower/sub bass frequencies reside under 200Hz. They provide *depth* and *fullness*. If the guitar is paired with an acoustic kickdrum, considering this frequency range is crucial due to the lack of sub bass in the kickdrum.

2. 200-350Hz is an area that requires attention. If your bass sounds *muddy*, try cutting this frequency range. If it lacks *power*, try enhancing this area.

3. 400-1000Hz gives your bass *presence* and *growl*. Increasing the amplitude of this area may give your bass more guttural *aggression*.

4. 2.5kHz-5kHz gives your bass some *bite* and *snap*. Remember, though, that boosting this area may compete with other instruments that occupy this range, such as percussion and leads.

The estimated frequency profile of a bass guitar is shown in Figure 3.7:

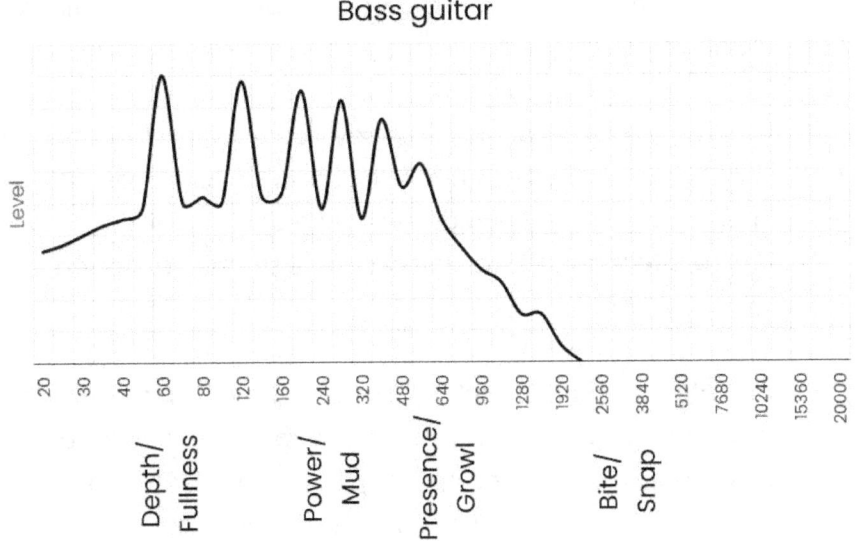

Figure 3.7: The estimated frequency profile of a bass guitar.

Now, we'll look at some percussion.

Open hi-hat

Open hi-hats are one of the most important percussive instruments. They can be difficult to get right, however. Even though they sound like high-frequency instruments, there's a lot of low and mid frequencies to contend with.

Areas to look out for

1. Hi-hats in drum machines, such as the 808 or 909, can contain some bass presence below 400Hz. This is often an unnecessary presence that takes up headroom, so you can filter this area out using a high-pass filter. Some producers who wish to give the hi-hat a more aggressive sound filter as low as 200Hz. Equally, other producers who

want the hi-hat to "sit" more comfortably in the mix filter higher.

2. Even though they sound like they occupy high frequencies only, the main *body* of the hi-hat can be as low as 900Hz. This area gives the hi-hat the sense of being struck. Too little presence in this area can make the hi-hat sound *weak* and *hollow*.

3. Hi-hats have significant *sibilance* in the 4-9kHz range. This is an area that requires caution, as too much *sibilance* can make the hi-hat sound grating. Some precise EQ to attenuate harsh *sibilances* in this area is sometimes necessary.

4. Finally, the hi-hat possesses some *sparkle* above 9kHz. To make the hi-hat stand out, focus on this frequency range, but be mindful of other instruments like cymbals, shakers, or vocals.

The estimated frequency profile of an open hi-hat is shown in Figure 3.8:

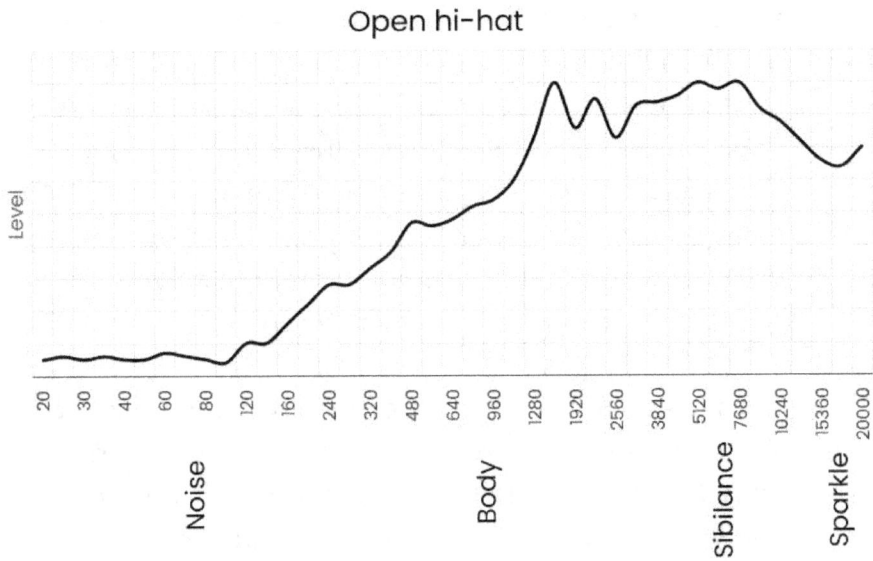

Figure 3.8: The estimated frequency profile of an open hi-hat.

Snare

Snare drums are another vital percussive instrument that can make or break a mix. Just like hi-hats, they are deceptive – even though they sound like a high-frequency instrument, they have a great deal of low and mid energy.

Areas to look out for

1. Snare drums have some *rumble* below 100Hz. You can normally get rid of this *rumble* without affecting the quality of the snare.

2. Snare drums possess a great deal of low end, with a particular *thud* between 120Hz and 400Hz. This is the *thud* you feel in your body when hearing a live band play a real

snare drum, and you can boost it if you want to boost the snare. Attenuating this area can make the snare sound hollow, but this is not a concern when you want the snare to sit above the mix, such as a supporting snare in a Tech House drum track. In electronic music, you may hear producers cut the *thud* part of the snare drum below 400Hz entirely, as it can interfere with the harmonics of the bass. Use your ears to judge whether this is right for you – as it sacrifices some of the realism of the snare.

3. The snare then has a *crack* between 1kHz and 6kHz. Too little of this frequency range, and the snare will sound muted, as if playing from another room. Too much of this, and your snare will sound sibilant and grating.

4. Finally, a snare has a *sparkle* from 7kHz to 20kHz, which you can boost if you want the snare to cut through the mix.

The estimated frequency profile of a snare is shown in Figure 3.9:

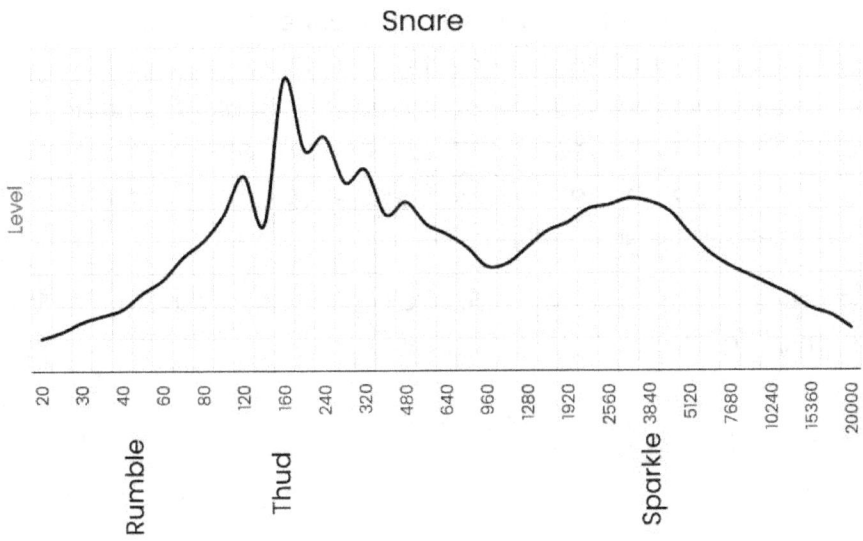

Figure 3.9: The estimated frequency profile of a snare drum.

Shaker/tambourine

The shaker and the tambourine have a similar frequency profile to one another. Their shuffling, noisy, slightly syncopated sound can add a great deal of energy to a track that's growing tiresome.

<u>Areas to look out for</u>

1. There is some noisy presence under 1kHz that, whilst adding a small amount of realism, can often be removed using a high-pass filter.

2. Shakers and tambourines both have some *body* between 1kHz and 4kHz. This imbues the instrument with realism and presence; presence that isn't always desirable in a mix.

3. The *sparkle* of a shaker or tambourine resides around 5kHz–15kHz. Many music producers use a shaker and/or a tambourine to add an energetic *sparkle* alone to their sound. Here, they roll off frequencies under 5kHz – but this comes at the cost of realism, making the instrument in isolation sound hollow.

The estimated frequency profile of a shaker and a tambourine is shown in Figure 3.10:

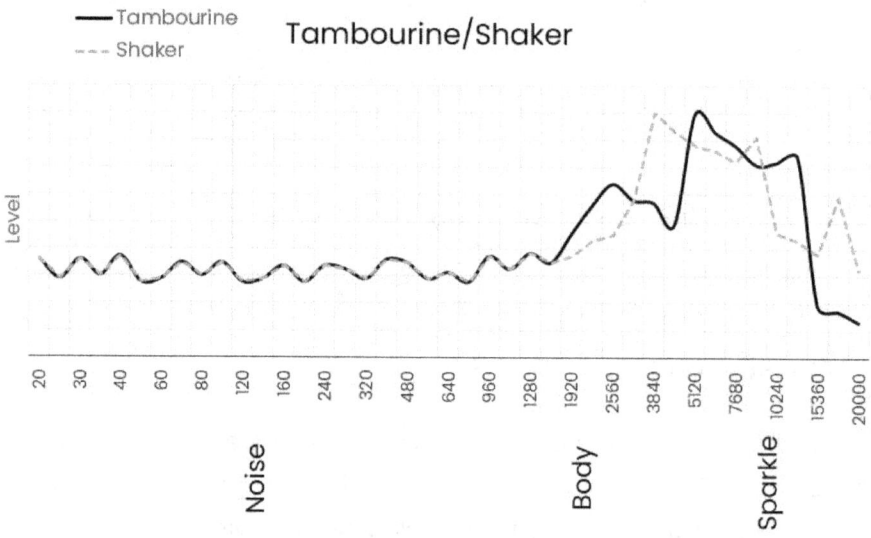

Figure 3.10: The estimated frequency profile of a tambourine and shaker.

Lead synthesizer

Lead synthesizers play the role of adding a textural focal point for the listener. When done right, they soar over the mix, bringing everything together. When done wrong, they weigh the mix down, with all elements sinking into the *mud* they create.

A monophonic lead synthesizer has two sets of harmonics - the initial harmonics (often five or so) and a denser set that decreases rapidly as the harmonics increase.

Areas to look out for

1. The lower harmonics, which tend to reside between 120 and 500Hz, give your lead *power*. If the fundamental frequency or lower harmonics of your lead conflict with your kick or your bassline, you will hear your mix become *muddy*. You can fix this by rolling off the lower harmonics gently with a high-pass or low-shelf filter to resolve the conflict. Like many other instruments, a lead can safely *float* on top of a mix if you so choose.

2. The higher harmonics, generally between 500Hz and 2kHz, give your lead *clarity* and *presence*. If your lead's filter has high Resonance, be careful - as boosting this area can sometimes create quite grating resonances.

3. *Sibilance* comes from the area between 2kHz and 10kHz. Depending on the type of lead, boosting this area can provide extra *clarity*, but may bring your lead into conflict with your higher percussion elements.

4. Finally, you may wish to consider using a low-pass filter above 10kHz or so, to define the top end of your lead in relation to your elements with more *sparkle*, such as tambourines.

The estimated frequency profile of a lead synthesizer is shown in Figure 3.11:

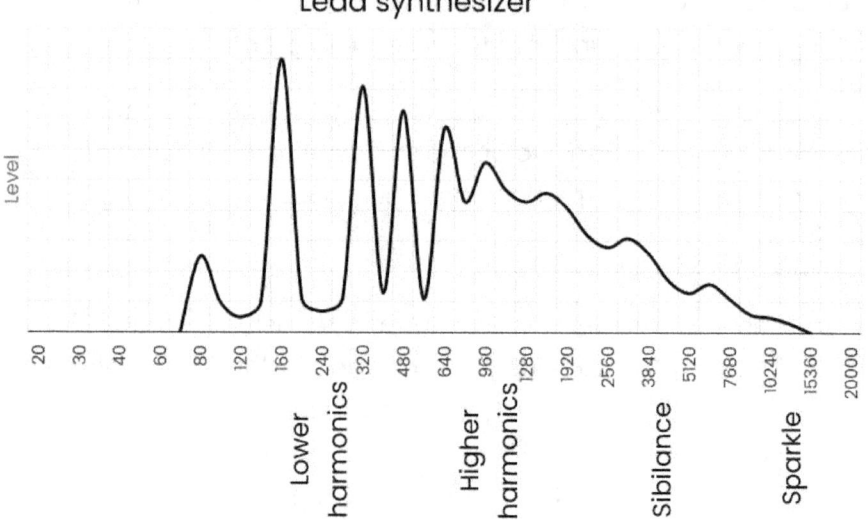

Figure 3.11: The estimated frequency profile of a lead synthesizer.

Pad

Pads, just like leads, can soar, tie elements together, or even give your listener goosebumps when done right. When done badly, their slow-moving timbre sucks the energy and life out of your mix.

Areas to look out for

1. Pads can often possess low-frequency *rumble* and *noise* below 200Hz, which you should consider removing with a high-pass filter unless this presence is intentional (for example in the introduction to a track, where the pad sits alone).

2. Pads have a great deal of *presence* in the 200Hz-500Hz range. If the pad is the centre of attention in your mix, this

can create a full, enveloping sound. However, this may conflict with your bass and create *mud* if the pad isn't meant to be the centre of attention. If you intend for your pad to add warm melody, without weighing down your mix and potentially drowning out your bass, you can use a high-pass filter to remove everything below 200-500Hz.

3. A lot of the more attention-grabbing elements of a pad comes from constructive and destructive interference of waveforms, sometimes described as *bite*. This is often found around 800Hz-2kHz.

4. From 2kHz to 10kHz, there is also a great deal of pleasant *resonance*, which, like in leads, can grate if boosted too much.

5. Finally, pads have *sparkle* from 10kHz upwards, which you can highlight if you want your pad to be attention-grabbing. You can filter this *sparkle* out if you want your pad to sit comfortably with other high-frequency areas, such as your shakers.

Some producers, particularly in bass music, use pads to create a subtle atmosphere, whilst trying to make the pad as unnoticeable as possible. Here, a low-pass filter above 1kHz and a high-pass filter below 200Hz dulls the pad's *bite*, *resonance* and *sparkle*, without causing any conflicts with the kickdrum.

The estimated frequency profile of a pad is shown in Figure 3.12:

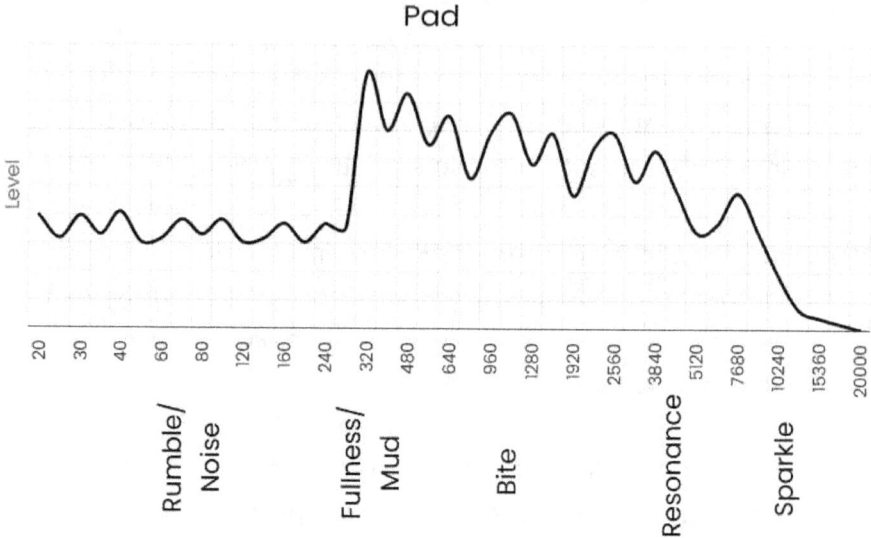

Figure 3.12: The estimated frequency profile of a pad.

Keys (e.g. Piano/Rhodes)

Keys are a great instrument to work with – they are the most evocative, funky, melodic instruments around. They must be treated fairly delicately to sound right, however.

Areas to look out for

1. Pianos and Rhodes contain *boominess* and bass around 20Hz to 200Hz. This can make the keys sound more realistic when they're the main focus, but it can clash with low frequency instruments in the mix. This area can be reduced in amplitude fairly safely if the keys should sit 'above' low-end instruments in the mix.

2. 200-500Hz can often contain the fundamental frequencies of many notes, but can add *mud* to the mix if emphasised too much. This area can also be reduced in amplitude slightly if necessary – the harmonics of the keys add a great deal to our perception of notes being played, meaning that presence from 200Hz to 500Hz isn't an absolute necessity for the listener's perception. It is, however, a good idea to keep some presence in this area to prevent the keys from sounding unrealistic.

3. 500-2kHz contains the main *bite* of the keys, which is an important element for our perception of the notes. If you remove the lower frequencies of the keys (particularly below 200Hz), the instrument can sound thin. You can compensate for this with a boost around 500-2kHz.

4. 2kHz-5kHz is where the *air* and *brilliance* reside. Boosting this area will bring the keys to the listener's attention due to it sounding bright.

5. Finally, 5kHz to 20kHz is where the *sparkle* of a piano resides.

An estimated frequency profile of a piano and Rhodes is shown in Figure 3.13:

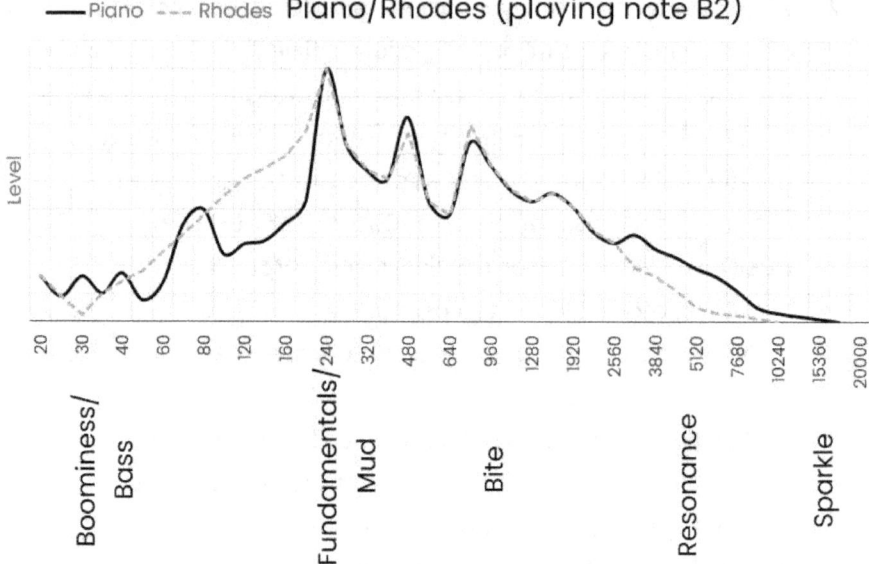

Figure 3.13: *The estimated frequency profile of a piano and a Rhodes piano.*

Vocals

Finally, vocals can be one of the more complex instruments to EQ. Vocal EQ can be complex because it depends on various factors such as the singer, the recording equipment, and the recording environment. Vocals are normally the main focal point of the track, however, and the most important element to get right!

Areas to look out for

1. The first area to pay attention to is the low-end *rumble* below 100Hz. Unless your singer is a bass singer, this will be rumble from the recording equipment, as well as other artefacts. This area should be cut significantly or eliminated using a high-pass filter.

2. The next area is around 100-350Hz and is often where the fundamental of the vocal resides. Too much emphasis on this area can lead to a *boomy* or *muddy* sound, but too little can make a vocal sound thin. If you're looking for background vocals to *float* in the mix, you can eliminate this area entirely with a high-pass filter.

3. A similar area can be found between 350 and 650Hz, where too much emphasis can lead to a *boxy* sound, whereas too little can also lead to *thinness*.

4. The mid-range of a vocal can be found between 800Hz and 4kHz. This is an area where your vocal can shine, but can also compete with lead instruments, hi-hats and snares for space. Sometimes a vocal can sound *nasal* and cutting around 800Hz to 1kHz can mitigate this. Boosting 1kHz-3kHz may increase the clarity of bass or tenor vocals, whereas boosting 2kHz-4kHz may increase the clarity of alto or soprano vocals.

5. *Sibilance*, the *sss* sound, is around 5kHz to 10kHz. This is where your vocal's *brightness* can be controlled, and any harsh, resonant *sibilance* can be fixed.

6. Finally, above 8kHz, is what we'd call *sparkle* - a subtle area that adds a special touch to your vocal.

The estimated frequency profile of vocals is shown in Figure 3.14:

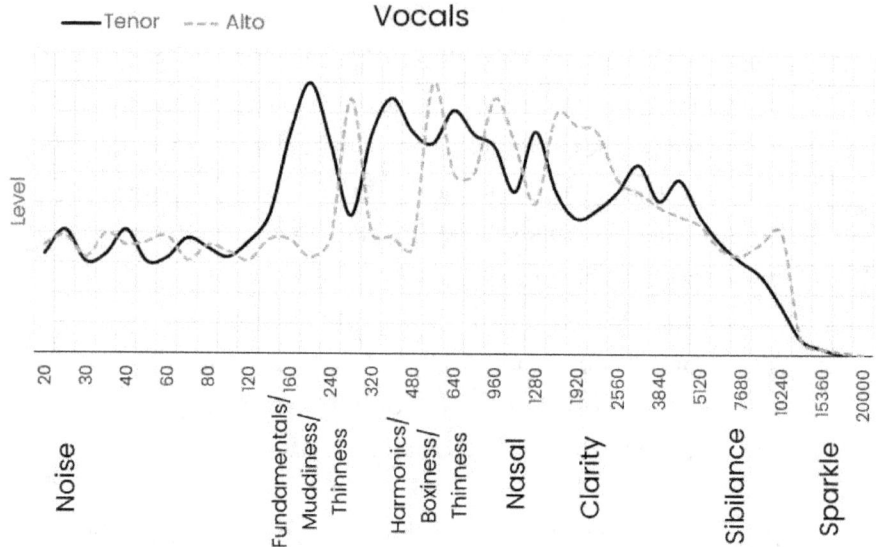

Figure 3.14: The estimated frequency profile of vocals.

Now that we've explored the basic frequency profile of some common instruments, let's explore EQ modules themselves. But first, some exercises to help you improve your understanding!

Exercises

1. Follow these instructions:
    a. Find an FFT Analyzer, either within your DAW or as a VST.
    b. Play a variety of instruments whilst observing their effect on the analyser, to give you some familiarity with the frequency spectrum. Observe for the fundamental and the harmonics.

2. Follow these instructions:

a. Load one of your favourite instruments or synth patches.
b. Record a MIDI clip of this instrument and play it back on a loop.
c. Then, add an EQ set to a notch filter.
d. Move this notch filter slowly up and down the frequency spectrum and listen carefully for how changes at particular frequencies affect the timbre of the instrument. Is there a frequency that makes the instrument sound *thin*? Or *boxy*? Or *muffled*?
e. Repeat this process for two more instruments.

Chapter 4: Types of EQ

After understanding EQ theory, let's compare the main types of EQ devices. There are three main types of EQ in use in music production: graphic, parametric, and semi-parametric. In this chapter, we shall explore them.

Graphic EQ

Graphic equalizers are a style of EQ commonly found in hardware devices. They comprise a set of filters, each fixed to a specific frequency range. These ranges are known as bands. The simplest example is found on basic DJ or analogue mixers, which offer three frequency bands: low, mid, and high; as shown in Figure 4.1:

Figure 4.1: The type of three-channel EQ found on DJ mixers.

Within DJ mixers, the low and high EQ pots are typically shelving filters, whereas the middle is a band-pass filter. Between the three, a reasonable amount of control of the entire frequency spectrum is possible, as shown in Figure 4.2:

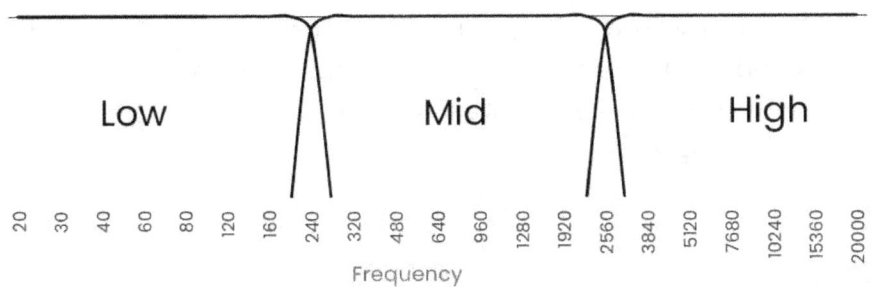

Figure 4.2: An example of the filtering found on three-channel EQ units within DJ mixers.

More complex examples of graphic EQ can be found on hardware devices such as stomp boxes, which often have between five and thirteen bands.

In studio equalizers, it's common to find devices with 31 bands. This is because each band corresponds to 1/3 of a musical octave. This is illustrated in Figure 4.3 below:

Figure 4.3: The filters on a 31-band studio EQ.

Despite being of relatively simple construction, many talented studio and live sound engineers do a great job with these graphic EQs. If you have to use one, you can still use your understanding of the frequency spectrum to gain decent results. However, in studio production, I would recommend using semi-parametric or parametric EQ where available. It is semi-parametric EQ that we shall explore next.

Semi-parametric EQ

Semi-parametric EQs offer a fixed number of filters (often three or four), but with the ability to select the crossover points between each band. The crossover points are where in the frequency range of one filter transitions into another. A semi-parametric EQ is illustrated in Figure 4.4:

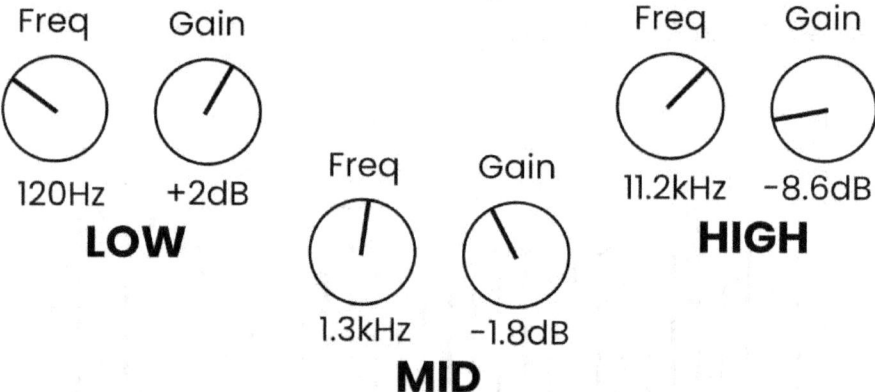

Figure 4.4: An example of a semi-parametric equalizer. Notice that whilst there are three bands, the frequency of each band is adjustable.

Some offer additional features, such as:

- A choice of filter types
- A distortion algorithm

- The ability to process either the centre, or the sides of the stereo image.

Even though they lack the flexibility of parametric EQs, semi-parametric plugins are still quite popular. This is because famous vintage EQs, regarded for their warm sound, tend to be semi-parametric. Semi-parametric plugins that are based on vintage hardware can be of exceptionally good sound quality and can command a high price.

Despite their commonality in hardware equipment, you are less likely to encounter and use a graphic or semi-parametric equalizer in DAW software. In DAW software, you are more likely to use a parametric equalizer - and it is this that we shall explore next.

Parametric EQ

Parametric equalizers are the most common type found in DAW software. Unlike graphic EQs, they offer the user complete flexibility as to:

- The number of filters in use
- The type of filters used
- Each filter's centre frequency/cut-off
- Each filter's Q value

An example, from Ableton Live's EQ Eight, is shown in Figure 4.5:

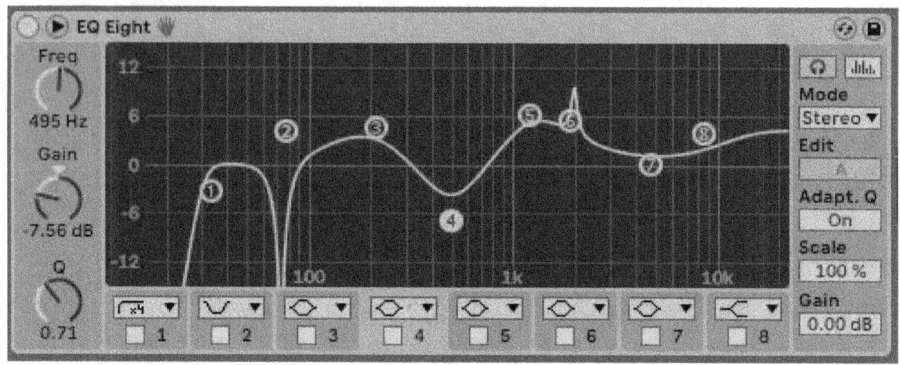

Figure 4.5: Ableton Live's EQ Eight, an example of a parametric equalizer.

Between the eight available filters, it's possible to create pretty much any reasonable EQ shape. Even though Parametric EQs lack the convenience of graphic equalizers, or the analogue warmth of hardware semi-parametric equalizers, their adaptability means that they are highly prevalent a digital studio environment.

Parametric EQ is the EQ type that we shall principally focus on in this book. Despite looking complex, it is easy to use. It is also far easier to adapt techniques learned on a Parametric EQ to other EQ types than it is to go from a Graphic EQ to a Parametric one.

Now that we understand types of EQ, let's look at the very basics of how to operate a Parametric EQ plugin.

Exercises

Answer these questions. If you get stuck, the answers are in the Appendix at the back of this book.

1. What type of EQ is most commonly found on DJ mixers?
2. What does the Frequency parameter do on semi-parametric EQ?

3. What's the difference between parametric EQ and semi-parametric EQ?

Chapter 5: How to Operate an EQ

This is a brief, but important chapter that will give you the fundamentals of how to operate EQ, beginning with Parametric EQ.

All professional-level DAW software usually has a Parametric EQ built in. In Ableton Live, it's called EQ Eight; in Logic Pro X, it's called Channel EQ; in Bitwig Studio, it's called EQ+. All parametric EQs look very similar, making it easy to move from one plugin to another without too much difficulty.

Let's look at a Parametric EQ element-by-element, beginning with the fundamental features. Ableton Live's EQ Eight is illustrated in Figure 5.1:

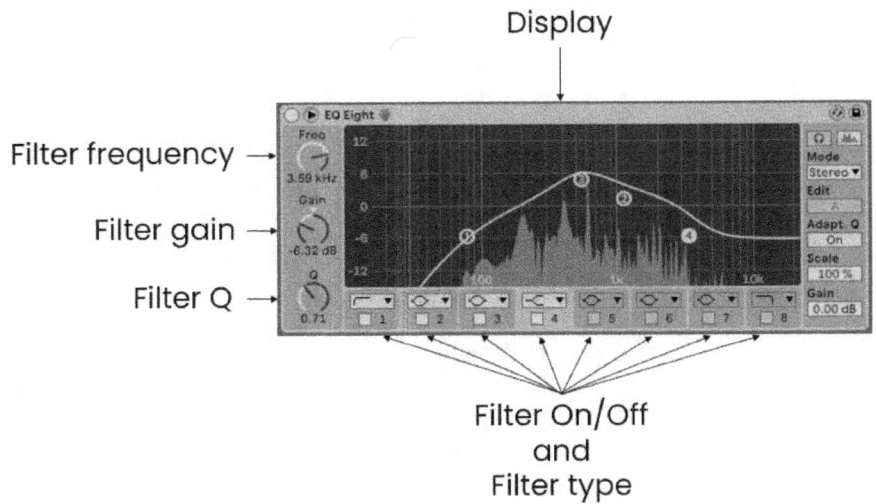

Figure 5.1: Ableton Live's EQ Eight with functions labelled.

The most important element is the **Display**. This shows you an FFT analysis of the audio input in the background, with the foreground showing each active filter. Some plugins allow you to choose whether the FFT analyses your audio input, or the audio output (i.e., the spectrum analysis of your sound after EQing).

The active filters combine to form the overall EQ curve, which is the line that runs horizontally across the screen. This curve defines the change that will happen to the amplitude of each frequency across the audio spectrum. For example, in Figure 5.1, a 10kHz tone would have its amplitude reduced by 6dB.

When the amplitude is increased or decreased by more than the screen's capacity (for example, Filter 1 is set to low-pass in Figure 5.1), the curve falls off the screen. This is because there is only a limited amount of space, and it's important that the detail of the EQ curve is captured. When a filter causes the curve to fall off the screen, you can safely infer what you can't see by continuing to draw the line mentally. An example of this is shown in Figure 5.2:

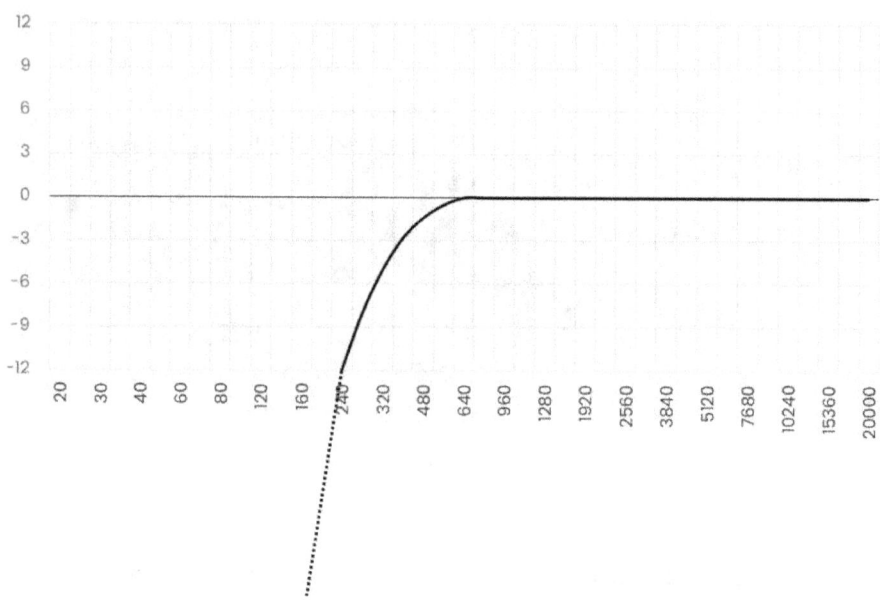

Figure 5.2: The imaginary EQ curve continues outside the displayed curve. When your parametric EQ line hits the bottom of the EQ device, it's helpful to imagine it continuing outside the device in such a fashion.

At the bottom of the plugin is the **Filter Selection** bank. This allows you to choose which filters are in use, and what type of filter is being used in each.

When you select a filter, the three parameters to the left of the plugin come into play:

- The filter **Frequency** is the cutoff/centre frequency (depending on the filter employed).
- The filter **Gain** is the relative increase or decrease of amplitude at that frequency.
- The filter **Q** is the filter Quality, as defined in Chapter 1.

Most DAW-based parametric plugins allow you to manipulate the filter with the computer mouse by dragging the point around. This is more intuitive than altering the frequency and gain of each filter with the pots.

Parametric EQ plugins also have a set of global parameters, as illustrated in Ableton Live's EQ Eight in Figure 5.3:

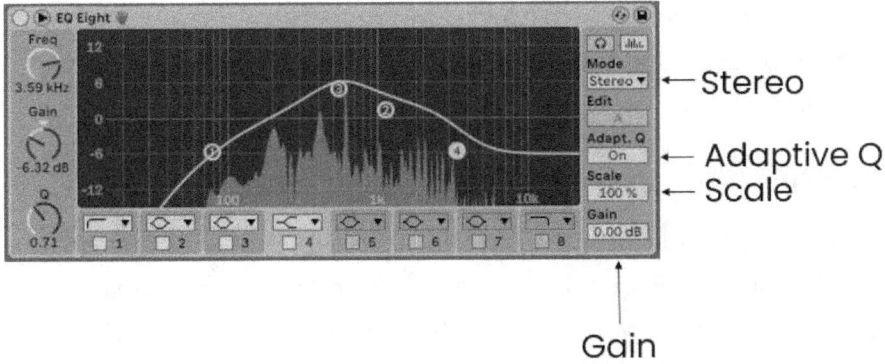

Figure 5.3: Ableton Live's EQ Eight, with its global parameters labelled.

- **Stereo** allows you to choose the stereo mode of the EQ. We'll look more at this towards the end of the book.
- **Adaptive Q** increases the Q in line with the extent of the boost of the cut. The bigger the boost or cut, the higher the Q, and therefore the narrower the bell filter. This can make using the EQ more intuitive, especially if you're using the Mouse on the display.
- **Scale** increases or decreases the amount of Gain on all filters, allowing you to test different degrees of increase or attenuation whilst maintaining the fundamental shape of the curve.
- **Gain** allows you to increase or decrease the amplitude of the output. This is useful to compensate for any amplitude gain or loss caused by EQ.

Despite the relative complexity of some elements of EQ, using a parametric EQ is highly intuitive. Simply:

1. Add the plugin to the channel you wish to apply EQ to.
2. Begin using the filters to shape your sound.

Now that you understand how to use parametric EQ, it should be easy to understand the use of semi-parametric EQ. Here's a primer.

Semi-parametric EQ

Using a semi-parametric EQ is slightly more challenging than a purely parametric one, because you usually can't see the EQ curve. You can, however, often infer it from the EQ's interface.

Look for the following features when inferring the parametric EQ's curve:

1. Symbols or text that tell you the type of filter (e.g., low-pass, high-shelf, bell). These will commonly look like the filters in Table 1.1 of Chapter 1. You can sometimes choose between different types.
2. Text to show whether the filters operate independently or whether you're controlling a *crossover*. If it's a *crossover*, changing the frequency changes the point at which one filter moves to the next one. If not, assume they work independently.
3. An option to control the Q of the filter. This will sometimes be a pot but will sometimes be a button that lets you decide whether to use *Hi-Q* mode or not. *Hi-Q* would increase the amount of Q.

An example of this is shown in Figure 5.4:

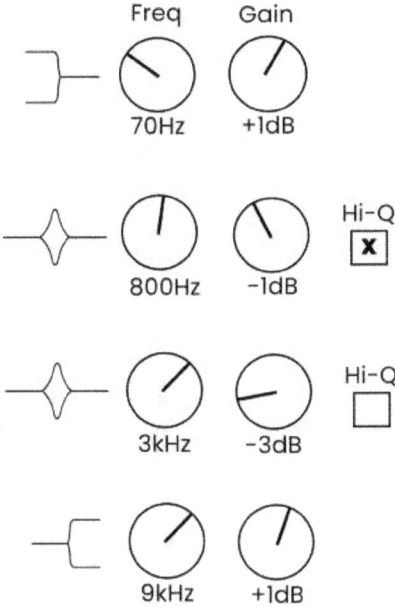

Figure 5.4: An example of semi-parametric EQ. Look out for the filter curves on the left, the parameters in the centre, and the Hi-Q buttons on both bell curves in the middle.

Using the filter type indicators, the frequencies chosen, the gain, and the Hi-Q buttons, we can infer the EQ curve. For example:

1. We can see that there is a low-shelf filter with the Frequency set to 70Hz, and the Gain set to +1dB.
2. There is a bell filter at 800Hz set to -1dB. The *Hi-Q* box is active, meaning that the Q factor will be high, and therefore the bell filter will be sharp.
3. There is another bell filter at 3kHz set to -3dB. With *Hi-Q* off, this will be a fairly soft filter.
4. There is a high-shelf filter at 9kHz, which adds 1dB to frequencies above 9kHz.

Using our understanding of filter theory, we can draw these four onto a theoretical parametric EQ curve, as shown in Figure 5.5 below:

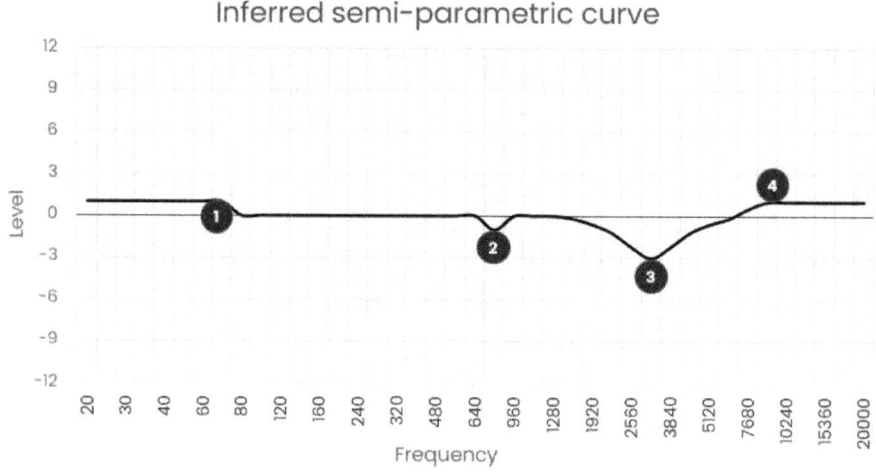

Figure 5.5: Inferred semi-parametric curve based on Figure 5.6 s parameters.

Remember, if you're struggling to infer an EQ's effect, you can always generate a pure white noise signal and visualise it using spectrum analysis. This will generate a flat frequency curve that will change shape according to your EQ's parameter changes.

Now that we've looked at the basics of using EQ, in the next chapter we'll look at some best practises.

Exercises

1. Open a DAW project file that you've been working on.

2. Add a parametric EQ to your master channel, experimenting with the various filters to hear their effect on your sound.
3. Use a semi-parametric EQ on a loop of white noise, adding an FFT plugin so that you can watch how your use of the EQ affects the frequency range.

Chapter 6: Practical EQ Tips

Before we look at real-world use of EQ, let's establish some fundamental ideas that will help you gain quick proficiency with EQ, saving you a great deal of time. The first is about understanding your aims.

Establish your aims!

Broadly, there are three reasons to use EQ:

1. Balancing. This is where you attenuate certain frequencies of a sound to make space for a competing element in your mix. An example of this is to attenuate the lowest end of a kick drum to create space for a sub bass.

2. Remove frequencies you don't want. This is where you attenuate certain frequencies of a sound because they don't sound good. A common example is to attenuate the *muddy* lower mid area of a pad sound.

3. Enhance frequencies you want. This is where you boost certain frequencies of a sound to bring them to a listener's attention - for example, a growling resonance on a Roland 303 bassline.

Sometimes, you're EQing for all three reasons. However, if you don't have a reason to use EQ, don't use it! Each EQ plugin in your mix adds another element of complexity that you must balance against other elements in your mix. Adding EQ to every single track forces you to consider mixing decisions not just in terms of each track, but each EQ added to each track – thus doubling the number of variables. It's perfectly acceptable to have tracks in your mix that have no EQ added to them – trust your ears and trust yourself!

Subtraction and addition

When you use EQ, you'll immediately notice two conflicting inclinations: to attenuate the frequencies you don't want, and to boost the frequencies you want.

To some extent, these are not mutually exclusive. Imagine that you wish to emphasise the frequencies under 1kHz in a sound. There are two ways you could do this:

1. A low shelf filter that increases the amplitude of frequencies under 1kHz (call this an additive approach, because you're adding to the amplitude of the overall sound).
2. A low shelf filter that reduces the amplitude of frequencies over 1kHz, then increasing the EQ's output gain (call this a subtractive approach).

These two approaches are compared in Figure 5.7 below:

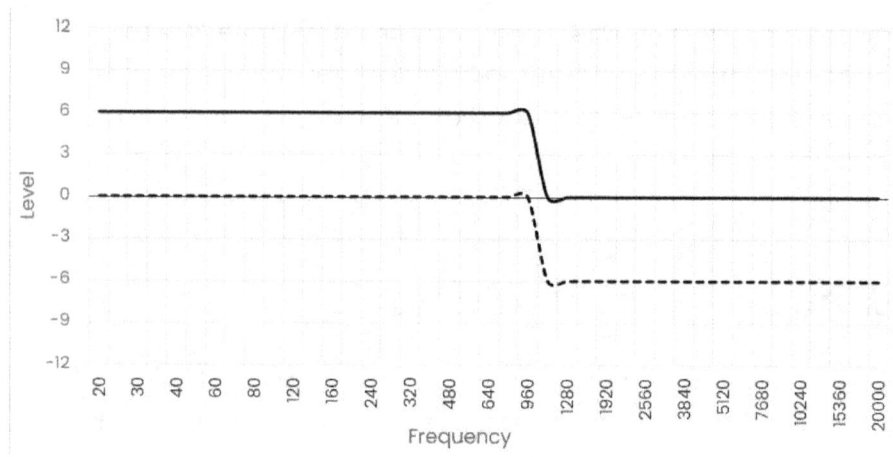

Figure 5.7: A subtractive EQ approach compared to an additive one.

As you can see, these two approaches create the same shape, and therefore, the same timbre. However, there's a limiting factor to consider: headroom. Headroom is the amount of room you can manoeuvre without pushing too much amplitude through your main output and creating undesirable distortion.

When you choose to *increase* the amplitude of a frequency, you increase that track's overall amplitude. This, in turn, reduces how much *more* amplitude you can add into your mix without generating distortion. This means that you'll have to adjust the other tracks in your mix to compensate for the headroom you've lost.

Therefore, it's far easier to use a subtractive approach where possible, as this won't cause the same sort of impact. Just remember to increase your EQ's output level to compensate for losing amplitude.

There are, of course, times when you'll want to boost a certain frequency without reducing the amplitude of other frequencies -

and that's fine. But when both additive and subtractive EQ give you the same result, choose subtractive.

Use EQ in context!

When using EQ, it's important to remember that your changes won't be heard in isolation - they will be heard in the context of your mix. Therefore, if you're using EQ to balance one element with another, it's important to make EQ changes with other elements of your mix playing. Believe me, I've wasted a long time EQing elements in *Solo*, only to discover that my changes are entirely incorrect with Solo switched off.

So, where possible, and particularly if you're balancing, make your adjustments without using *Solo*. If you find this means you can't hear your adjustments, bring the level of the track you're working on up, then back down once you've made your adjustments. If you must use *Solo*, un-*Solo* the layer you're working on regularly to make sure it works in context.

Otherwise, if you're using EQ to shape the timbre of an instrument and you don't care about the context, be aware that you may need to shape the surrounding elements in the mix.

Scanning for frequencies

Whilst the broad-brush frequency ranges in this book are a great way to know where to target for results, you'll need to locate the exact location of particular sounds or resonances. To do this, you'll need to learn to scan for frequencies. This is how you do this.

1. Let's say that you can hear a nasty resonance that you suspect to be somewhere in the mid-range, around 1kHz to 5kHz. First, increase the amplitude of this range significantly (at least 6dB), with a low degree of Q, to highlight it broadly. You should hear it increase in amplitude. This is shown in Figure 5.8:

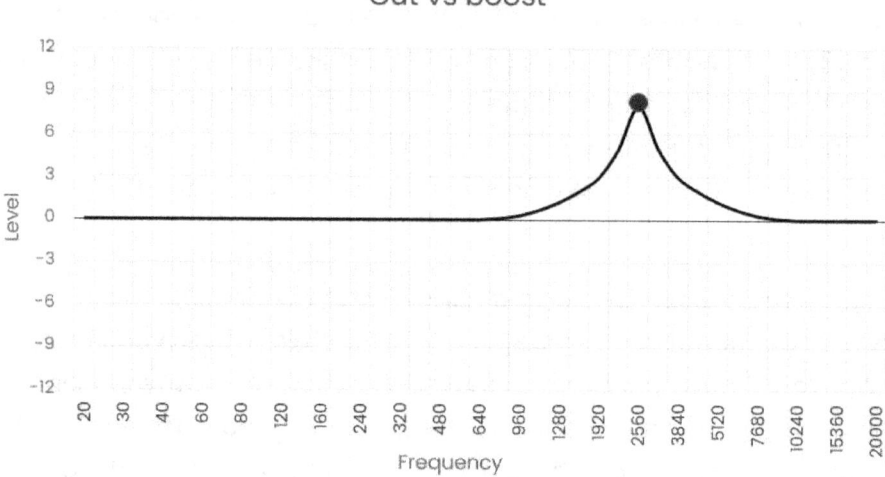

Figure 5.8: A significant increase in amplitude using a bell filter to search for a problem frequency.

1. Now, increase the Q significantly, so that only a small section of the frequency range is highlighted, as shown in Figure 5.9:

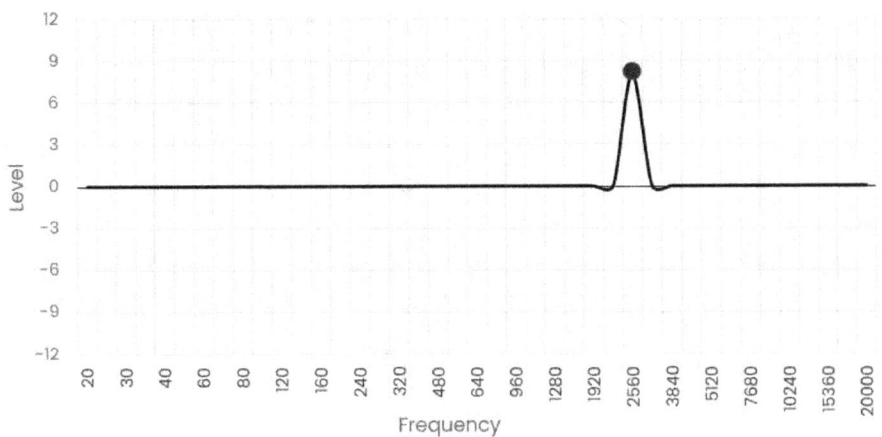

Figure 5.9: A bell filter with a high Q to highlight a tiny frequency range.

2. Sweep the *Frequency* parameter up and down until you hear your resonance. It should seem to pop out, as illustrated in Figure 5.10:

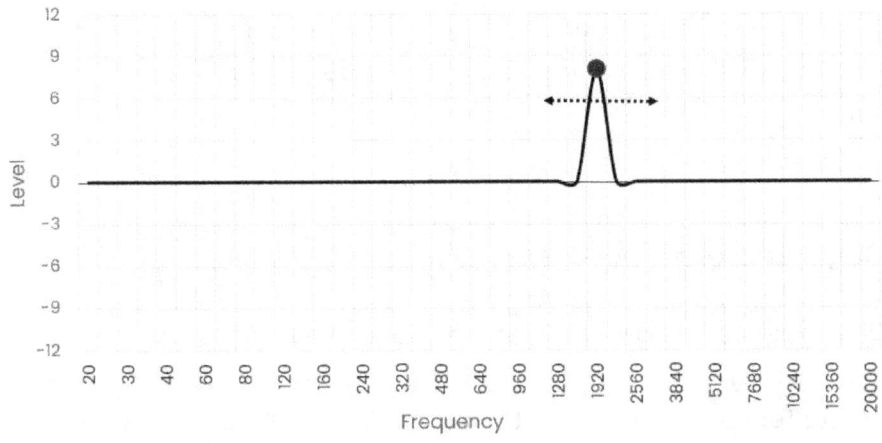

Figure 5.10: Sweeping the Frequency parameter up and down to find a problem frequency.

3. Attenuate this resonance to your liking, and then increase and decrease the Q until you're satisfied that the

resonance has been attenuated enough. The final attenuation is shown in Figure 5.11:

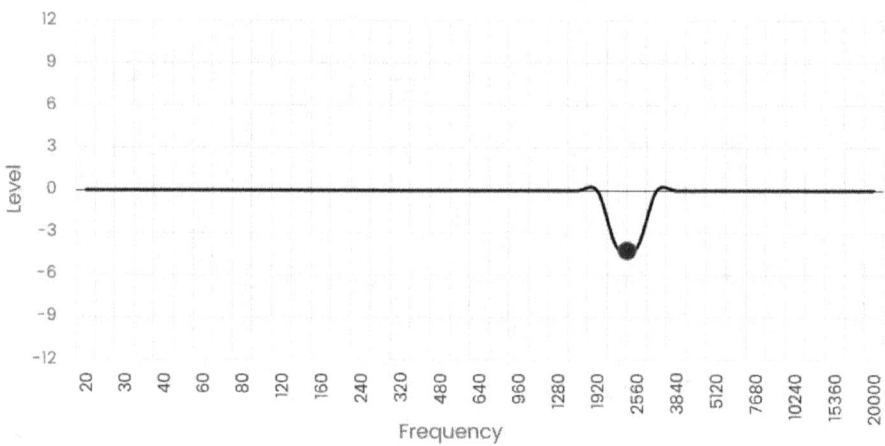

Figure 5.11: The attenuation of the problem frequency.

You can use this 'scanning' technique for a lot of purposes – you could, for example, use it to hear the constituent parts of a new instrument, or to find out areas of conflict in your mix. To summarise, this 'scanning' technique should become part of your day-to-day mixing method.

Don't use presets!

Whilst there's no harm in listening to EQ presets to hear how other sound designers have used EQ, the designers of presets can't hear the context of your mix, can't hear the timbre of the instrument you're using, and they don't know your aims. Use your ears, your knowledge of the frequency range, and the scanning technique detailed above to decide, instead. Even if you have little experience of using EQ, you will achieve better results by designing your own EQ curves.

Now that we've looked at some broad principles to use when applying EQ, let's next explore some real-world examples of EQ use. But first, some exercises!

Exercises

Answer these questions. If you get stuck, the answers are in the Appendix at the back of this book.

1. Why is using an EQ preset a bad idea?
2. Why should you normally subtract, instead of adding frequencies?
3. Why shouldn't you simply EQ every track in your mix?

Follow these instructions:

    a. Open one of your DAW project files. Add a parametric EQ to a prominent channel (for example a lead, or a prominent drum layer).
    b. Increase the amplitude of this element above 1kHz using a low-shelf filter. To do this, you have to EQ subtractively.
    c. Write a drum track that covers most of the frequency spectrum (i.e., including a kick, snare, and hi-hat at minimum). Bring this drum track's amplitude down by 6dB using your mixer. Then, use the frequency scanning technique to sweep up and down the frequency spectrum using a narrow bell filter. Listen for the resonances that jump out. Don't have your monitors or headphones too loud for this exercise, as there can be some strong resonances!

Chapter 7: Real EQ Use: Shaping

In this chapter, we'll look at some practical examples of EQ in action. I'll show you four real-world examples of EQ that I've used in tracks, and in the exercises, I'll ask you to create four examples of your own.

You can download my examples here:
https://eq.producers.guide

But first – if you're struggling with EQ, let's consider what shaping is, and why you'd want to do it. What do you do if you don't know *how* you want to shape your sound?

Thankfully, it's quite simple!

1. Listen to your sound. Do so critically and honestly.
2. What's it lacking? *Power*? *Presence*? *Sparkle*?
3. What's wrong with it? Is it *weak*? *Muddy*? *Grating*?
4. If you're happy with the sound having critically analysed it, it doesn't need EQing!
5. If you're not happy, use your knowledge of the frequency spectrum from Chapters 2 and 3 to know what to adjust, and where. For example, power comes from the sub bass and bass range; *presence* or *muddiness* comes from the low mid and mid range, *grating* and *sparkle* comes from the upper mid and high end.

Let's look at some individual examples.

A solo Roland 303

I was working on a track that was underpinned by a Roland 303 bassline – a typical, classic, Acid sound. My problem was that whereas normally a 303 is supported by a strong kickdrum, I didn't want a kick in this track. In this case, the 303 had to take control of the entire low end of the track.

A Roland 303 is a unique synthesizer to work with. Its distinctive filter creates a warm, rubbery sound – a sound which has underpinned thousands of electronic music tracks since its release in 1981.

If it's playing without a kick, we need to emphasise its fantastic sound, whilst adapting to some of the tonal imbalances found in the synthesizer.

One of these tonal imbalances is a lack of presence in the sub bass range. The first step is therefore to boost the sub-bass frequency range under 80Hz. This can be accomplished most easily with a low-shelf filter that increases the amplitude of the sub-bass area like that of a kickdrum, but maintains a balance, as the low-shelf filter is a straight line.

Then, it's worth considering the low mids. Whilst these contribute to a lot of warmth in a 303, they are very loud, and can sound *muddy*. Here, it is therefore appropriate to attenuate these frequencies.

Next, the mids on a Roland 303 can sound *boxy* in a mix, therefore attenuating these can help mitigate this *boxiness*. Here, around 480Hz was the right point after some scanning.

Finally, the top end, around 5kHz and above, is an area that doesn't usually feature significantly on bass synthesizers – however, thanks to the resonance on a 303's filter, there is some small amount of *sparkle*. This *sparkle* can be helpful if you want the 303 to be front and centre of the mix, but if you wish for it to underpin the track then it's prudent to attenuate this frequency range slightly, as shown in Figure 7.1:

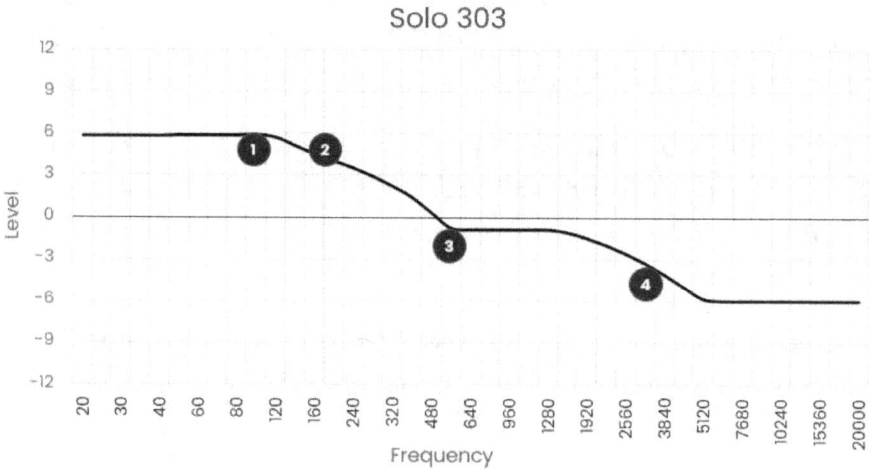

Figure 7.1: *An example EQ curve used on a Roland 303.*

A wispy cymbal

Like many producers who write Techno, I love using wispy cymbals part-way through a track. They hover over the mix, adding extra high-end energy and *sparkle* when an arrangement is becoming stale. You can hear them regularly in House, Tech House, and drum and bass.

Equally, subtle crash cymbals can add rhythmic interest to an arrangement without interrupting the sound with a huge *crash*.

The problem is that stock cymbals, particularly the routinely used 909 ride and crash, have a fairly wide frequency range. This prevents the cymbal from sitting comfortably on top of the mix.

The best results come from using a low-pass filter and a high-pass filter together. Setting a low-pass filter around 8kHz means that the highest *sparkle* of the frequency range is removed, preventing the cymbal from grabbing excessive attention by dominating the very top end of the mix. Then, a high-pass filter around 3kHz prevents the noisy middling frequencies of the cymbal from conflicting with the *body* of the hi-hats and snares. You'll notice that these two filters in tandem can create a small peak around 4kHz - there's no harm in this.

You can also use this technique for other instruments that you wish to sit on top of the mix, such as sound effects, or subtle whispered vocals. The final EQ curve is shown in Figure 7.2:

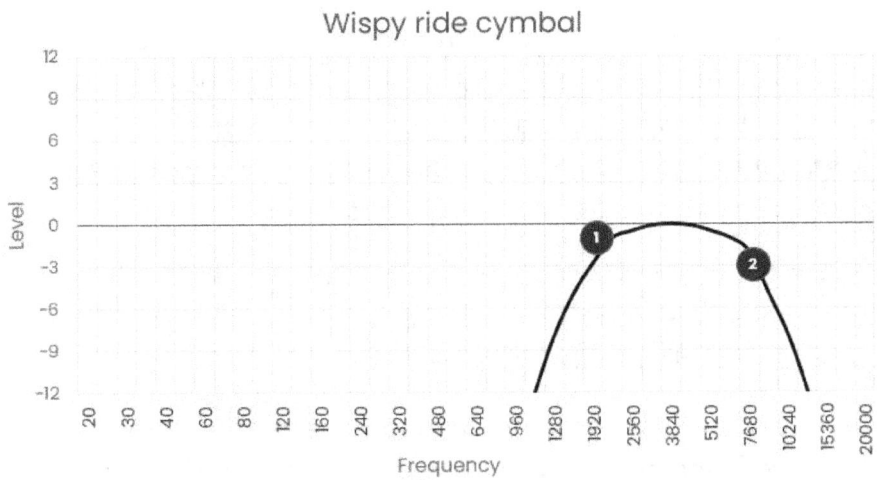

Figure 7.2: An example EQ curve used on a 909 ride cymbal to create a wispy sound that seems to sit above the mix.

A piano

A piano is a great instrument to add to a track. It adds soul, melody, expressiveness, and harmonics.

Despite this, pianos can be a challenging instrument to EQ. Part of their beauty comes from the wide frequency range they occupy, as well as the interesting timbre that comes from a real instrument being played – the gentle *boom* of keys being hit, the reverberations of the piano strings, and the resonances of the materials that the instrument is made from. These combine to create a unique sound – but one that is difficult to EQ.

Therefore, a good start when EQing a piano is to consider where these elements sit on the frequency range:

1. The fundamental bass notes that provide the *body*.
2. The *bite* of the higher notes.
3. The *air* that gives the piano its *brilliance*.

In a track that I worked on, the fundamentals of the bass notes were around 150Hz, and the *rumble* below this frequency added nothing to the overall sound. Therefore, it was appropriate to increase the amplitude of the area around 150Hz, and to cut the frequencies below 150Hz with a high-pass filter.

The *bite* of the higher notes was around 2kHz – towards the upper end of where this would be expected, and boosting this area added a great deal to the piano's sound.

The *air*, in this case, was found around 8kHz, and increasing the amplitude of the piano in this frequency area made it shine.

Significantly attenuating the areas between these three key areas altered the tonal balance of the piano. The best results therefore came from allowing these to attenuate as part of the overall EQ curve. The final EQ curve is illustrated in Figure 7.3:

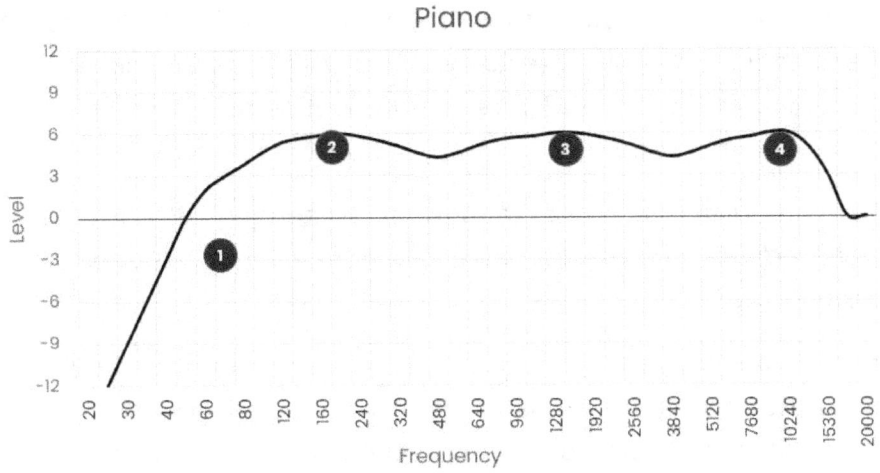

Figure 7.3: An example EQ curve used on a piano.

A pad

I sometimes use pads in my work for a variety of reasons. Pads have universally melodic, soaring qualities – but EQing a pad can depend on your aims for it.

In some tracks, the pad may add a melodic atmosphere and *depth*, yet be almost imperceptible to the listener. Here, a low-pass filter may prevent the pad from conflicting with the instruments at the front and centre of the mix (such as vocals or leads). In other tracks, the pad may be used as a melodic instrument that sits high in the mix. Here, a high-pass filter may prevent the pad from conflicting with the bass instruments.

In my case, I wanted a pad to sit gently in the mix, with some low-mid presence. Therefore, my first step when EQing a pad was to attenuate the low-end *mud*. I used my ear to evaluate where the high-pass filter should sit, but this will usually be between 300Hz and 600Hz. Broadly, a high-pass filter with a sharp roll-off (e.g.,

48dB/oct) will eliminate this low-end *mud*, whereas a high-pass filter with a gentle roll-off (e.g., 12dB/oct) will still give the listener the feeling of this low-end presence without adding too much *mud* to the mix. In this case, I chose a 12db/oct roll-off.

There are rare cases where this low-end is needed – in this case, the *muddiness* can be controlled in the mix using a low-shelf filter to attenuate it.

My next step was look for peaks on the spectrum analyser to find where the pad's *bite* is – this will usually be caused by constructive and destructive interference between the pad's detuned waveforms. There wasn't anything obvious on the analyser, so I used the 'scanning' technique until I heard a resonant peak. Much of the magic of the pad resides in this *bite*, so you should look to increase its amplitude to highlight it to the listener. This is usually around 800Hz to 2kHz.

I then wished to highlight the filter resonances around 2kHz-5kHz. I could, of course, attenuate this area if I wanted to move the pad further back in the mix. However, in this case, a bell filter with a low Q set to around +2dB highlighted these resonances well.

Finally, the pad's *sparkle*, around 5kHz-10kHz, could be enhanced – but only do this if your pad is front and centre of the mix. In my case it was, but the low Q bell filter around 5kHz achieved this. The final EQ curve is illustrated in Figure 7.4:

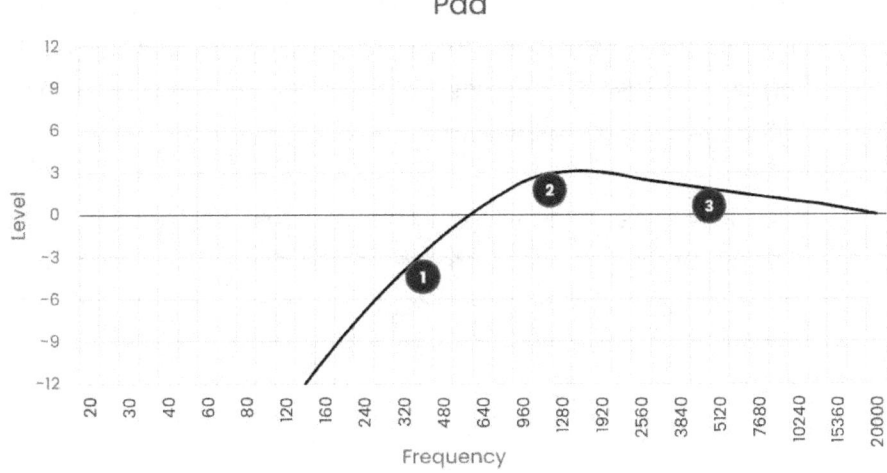

Figure 7.4: An example EQ curve used to shape a pad.

Now that we have reviewed isolated examples of using EQ to shape individual sounds, in the next chapter we shall explore using EQ to balance one or more sounds. But first, it's your turn to consolidate your knowledge of shaping.

Exercises

1. Create the following from your favourite DAW softsynth. Use EQ to attenuate an area you don't like, and highlight an area you do like:
    a. Bassline
    b. Pad
    c. Lead

2. Write a percussion track using a hi-hat and a clap. Use EQ to attenuate an area you don't like and highlight an area you do like.

3. Load a drum break sample. Make sure it's one you have a license for, because it came with your DAW, or it's licensed under Creative Commons. Enhance this drum break using EQ to make it more powerful. Look out for:

    a. Where the lower end adds *power*.
    b. Where the mids create *presence*.
    c. Where the high end adds *sparkle*.

Chapter 8: Real EQ Use: Balancing

Now that we've considered the use of EQ to shape sounds, let's look at the use of EQ to balance one or more sounds. This chapter offers four real-world examples of this. At the end of the chapter, I will ask you to create four real-world examples of your own.

You can download audio files of my examples here:
https://eq.producers.guide

Balancing can be more challenging than shaping, because balancing must take into context other layers. However, it's easy to get started.

Think of your mix like a family photograph at a wedding, or a class photograph at graduation. People in the front and centre of the photo might be more noticeable, while others could be towards the back and sides. However, everyone's faces are clear and identifiable. If someone is obscured behind someone else, the photographer will move them elsewhere so that they're in the camera frame.

This is the core purpose of balancing – giving instruments their place in the mix. If you don't, they can obscure one another and create a murky, opaque mix.

How do you know if instruments are in conflict? There are tell-tale signs:

1. Distortion, typically a *fuzzy* sound caused by too much amplitude at a particular frequency range.

2. A lack of clarity at one end of an instrument's frequency range.

3. A lethargic, *muddy* sounding mix, where individual elements don't sound clear.

Thankfully, balancing is simple – find out where the conflict is happening and decide which of your instruments will take precedence in that area.

FFT can help you find out where this conflict is. For example, look at these two FFT charts in Figure 8.1:

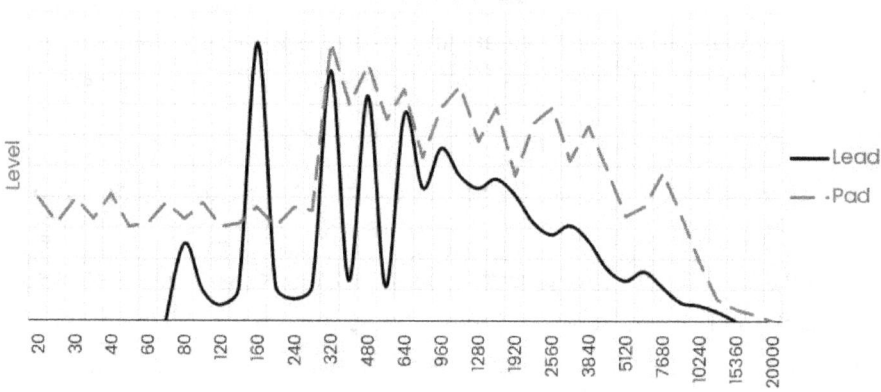

Figure 8.1: *A lead and a pad FFT analysis together.*

You can see that both the lead and pad peak between 320Hz and 800Hz. This is a typical example of such a conflict, and one that will be readily audible in your mix. You would therefore need to balance these two elements, usually by decreasing the amplitude of one of these two elements in the frequency area of conflict.

Let's have a look at four common scenarios where such a conflict may occur.

A kick and a sub bass

Combining a kick with a sub bass is one of the most common mixing challenges, and one of the most common uses of EQ. It is also one of the most delicate, given that these elements take up a huge amount of the headroom of your mix, and can easily sound poor if not correctly balanced.

When looking at individual instrument profiles, a kick and a sub bass each have two areas that clash:

1. The sub bass area below 80Hz. This is where your kick and sub bass's fundamental frequency both reside.

2. The bass area between 100Hz and 225Hz. This is where your kick's *thump* and your sub bass's harmonics reside.

Application of EQ is therefore simple in theory: you need to decide which instrument will occupy each of these two frequency bands. For the mix to sound right, one should occupy each frequency band.

If you choose for your sub bass to occupy the sub-bass area, your kick will sound like it sits on top of your sub bass. This is more common in genres like Dubstep or Drum and Bass.

If you choose for your kick to occupy the sub bass area, your sub bass will have a harmonic presence, but will have less chest-rattling energy on a big club system - however, your kick will sound powerful. This is more common in genres like Techno.

On this basis, a good starting point is to make a boost and a cut according to which element will sit above the other. Look for the fundamental and harmonics of each track, then boost one and cut another. For example, if the fundamental of your kick and sub bass are both around 50-60Hz, you could increase the amplitude of the sub bass and decrease the amplitude of the kick in this area. Given that this weakens your kick, you can apply the *opposite* effect with your harmonics, increasing the amplitude of the kick's harmonics around 100-400Hz (the *thump* and *harmonics*),

Finally, if you want both the kick and the bass to have equal prominence, you will need to use sidechain compression, so that the bass *ducks* in amplitude in response to the kick. I discuss this in my book entitled The Music Producer's Guide to Compression, but a starting point is to add a compressor to your bass, using your kick as a sidechain source, as shown in Figure 8.2:

Figure 8.2: Sidechain compression in Ableton Live's Compressor.

Sometimes, even after balancing the kick and sub bass correctly, both in terms of level and EQ, they still don't sound right together. Here, look critically at whether your kick is tuned to the same fundamental frequency as your bass (or at least a harmonic equivalent, e.g., seven semitones up). If that doesn't work, try swapping your kick for another. Sometimes the issue is a sound selection one, and no amount of EQ can rescue you!

Figure 8.3 and Figure 8.4 show an example of balancing a kick and bass. Here, the kick has been given prominence in the *thump* area, but the sub bass has been given prominence in the sub bass range. The harmonics of the bass have also been enhanced.

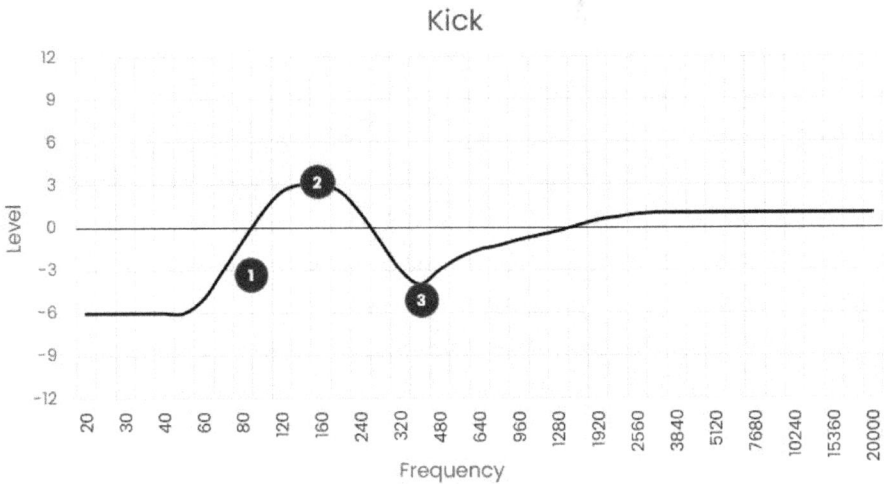

Figure 8.3: *An example of EQ use to balance a kickdrum with a sub bass.*

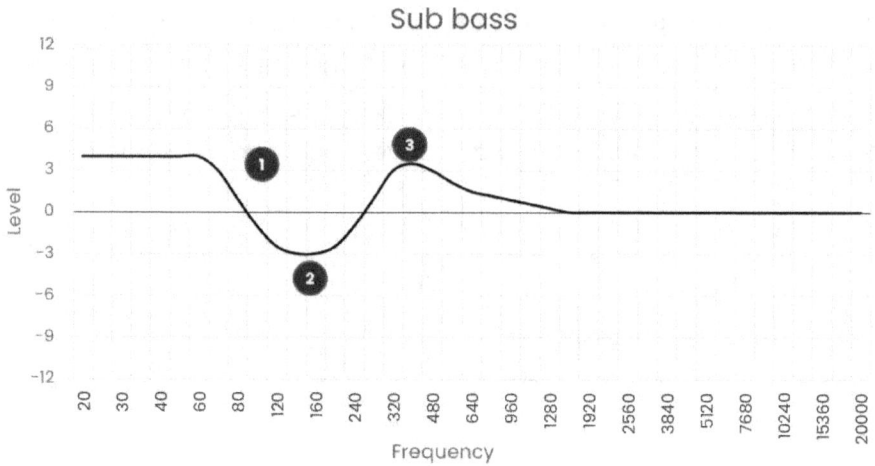

Figure 8.4: An example of EQ used to balance a sub bass with a kickdrum.

A stab and a bassline

Another common conflict you'll come across is between a bassline and a synth stab (or any other instrument in this range, for example, a pad, guitar, or piano). This conflict will happen around the middle-upper harmonics of the bass, leading to a *muddy* mix.

Whereas balancing a kick and a sub bass requires subtle tweaks, given their importance to the overall balance of the mix, you can be more brutal when working with these two melodic elements.

Personally, I prefer the warm, smooth harmonics of a bass to lower-end *mud* from a pad or stab. Therefore, a good starting point is to use a high-pass filter to eliminate the lower end of the pad (around 400Hz) entirely. This leaves space to increase the amplitude of the bass's harmonics. You can then add some clarity to the pad by boosting around 1kHz, but cut some of the noise by curtailing the top end with a harsh low-pass filter.

Sometimes, the lower end of a melodic instrument is required - for example, when working with instruments such as an electric piano. Here, you can still cut some of the 100-400Hz *mud*. To compensate for this cut, look for the harmonics of the lower notes, and boost these. This tells the listener that the notes are there, but without *muddying* up the mix too much.

The degree of tweaking required for the bass depends on its timbre. Sometimes, the bass requires very little EQ. This is because the harmonics of the bass do not cause significant conflict with the stabs. In other cases, such as when using a harsh bass, attenuation may be required around 1kHz to ensure that the warmth of the stabs is prominent.

The final EQ curves are illustrated in Figure 8.5 and Figure 8.6:

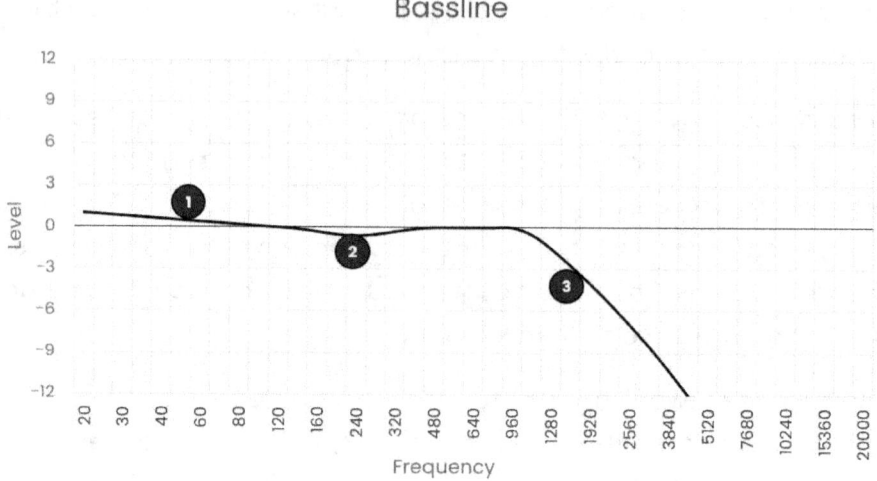

Figure 8.5: An example of EQ used to balance a bassline with stabs.

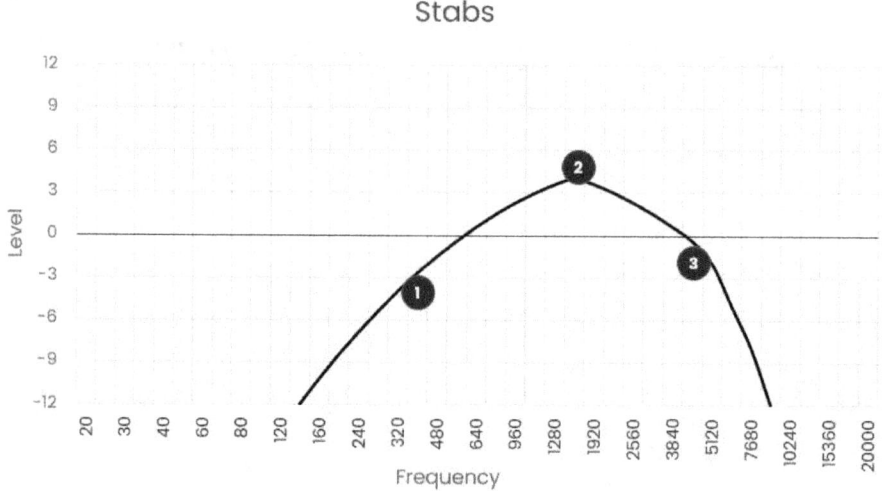

Figure 8.6: An example of EQ used to balance stabs with a bassline.

A snare and hi-hat

EQing your snare and hi-hat correctly is vital to give your mix *depth* and *clarity*. Whilst frequency clashes between these are less important (as the timing of the drums often separates them), carving out the correct amount of frequency space so that they sit comfortably together in the mix is vital.

Depending on the other elements in the mix, you may wish to add a gentle low-pass filter to roll off the lower frequencies of your snare, ensuring that ample space is created in the mix for the lower end of other instruments. Then, you can look for any awkward resonances using the Frequency Scanning technique.

With your snare EQed, you can look at the hi-hat. It can be tempting to imbue the hi-hat with *sparkle* by boosting the top end - but this doesn't always add the clarity that you want. A lot of clarity can be added by removing the *muddy* low end. To do this, set a high-pass filter, and gently increase the frequency until you reach the right spot. You'll probably find that if your high-pass filter is set too high, the hi-hats will sound 'pinched', so dial back slightly if you reach that point.

Awkward resonances are not unheard of in hi-hats either, so if the hi-hats have a grating sound, use the Frequency Scanning technique to find those difficult frequencies. If they are all above a certain threshold (e.g., 8kHz), they can be gently attenuated using a high-shelf filter.

An example of two EQ curves is shown in Figure 8.7 and Figure 8.8.

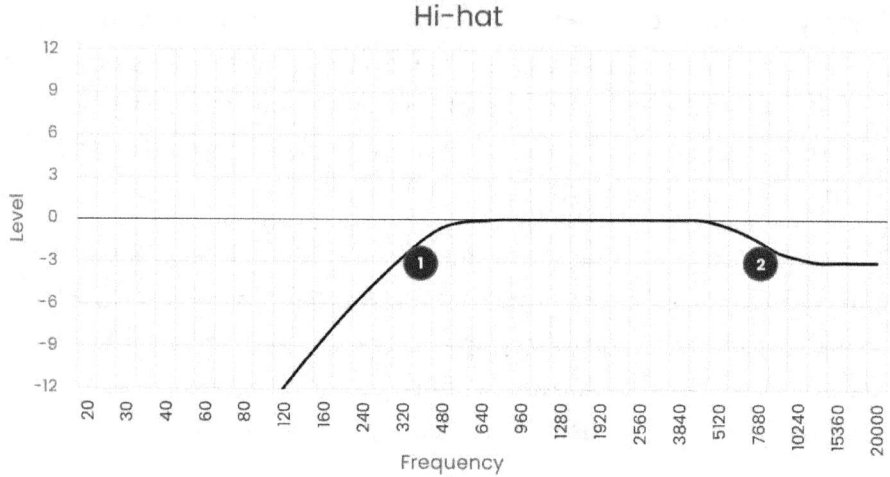

Figure 8.7: An example of EQ used to balance a hi-hat with a snare.

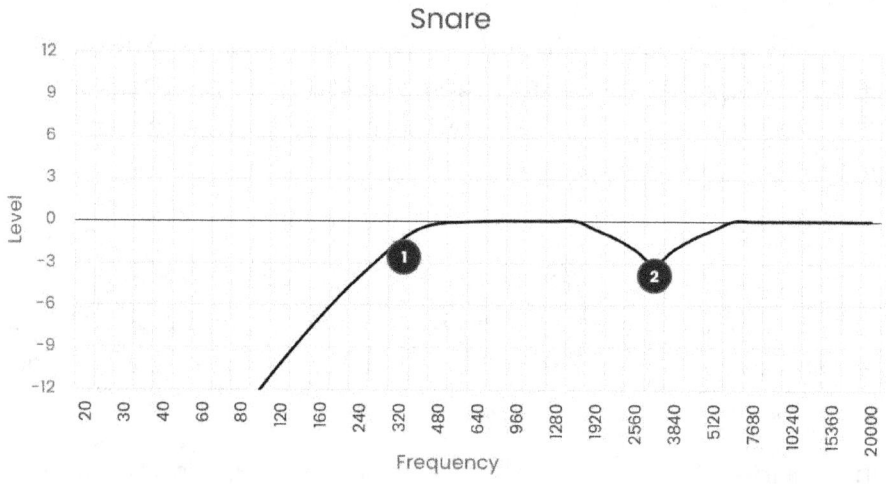

Figure 8.8: An example of EQ used to balance a snare with a hi-hat.

A whole track

For the last example of this chapter, I'd like to walk you through my EQ use on a real track that I released, one entitled Nonlinear Dynamics. Segmenting the track by the frequency ranges of the layers broke the mix down into five layers:

1. The kick
2. The bass
3. The chords (composed of two layers of chords)
4. The ride cymbal
5. The remaining percussion (composed of a hi-hat layer and a shaker with some Erosion applied for extra noise)

If you want to experiment with EQing this track yourself, I've made the stems available at https://eq.producers.guide/. There is also a loop of the mix with and without EQ available.

To begin with, listening to the mix, I noticed four distinct issues:

1. The bass was *boomy*, and it had a poor relationship with the kick. The two elements together lacked *tightness*. The bass also had pleasant mid harmonics that could be emphasised.
2. The chords were *muddy*, and they took up too much of the bottom end. They also had some nice *crunch* but sounded a tad on the *boxy* side. There was a bit too much *sparkle* when the filter opened.
3. The ride cymbal didn't *float* as I'd like it to.
4. The hi-hats and shaker had an irritating *resonance*, drawing too much attention to themselves.

Let's work through these issues step-by-step.

Firstly, I made the bass work with the kick. I did so by experimenting with the three setups set out earlier in this Chapter:

    a. The bass *below* the kick

b. The bass *above* the kick
c. Both bass and kick equal

I found that the most effective solution was for the bass to sit under the kick. Therefore, I emphasised the sub bass range of the bass, attenuating some of its harmonics that would occupy the same space as the *thump* of the kick. Then, I attenuated the sub bass range of the kick and emphasised the *thump* area.

The bass had some pleasant harmonics in the lower mid range, which I emphasised, whilst attenuating the same area of the kick.

The kick was slightly lacking in clarity, and so I therefore emphasised the *click* of the kick, at around 1kHz. Both EQ curves are shown in Figure 8.9:

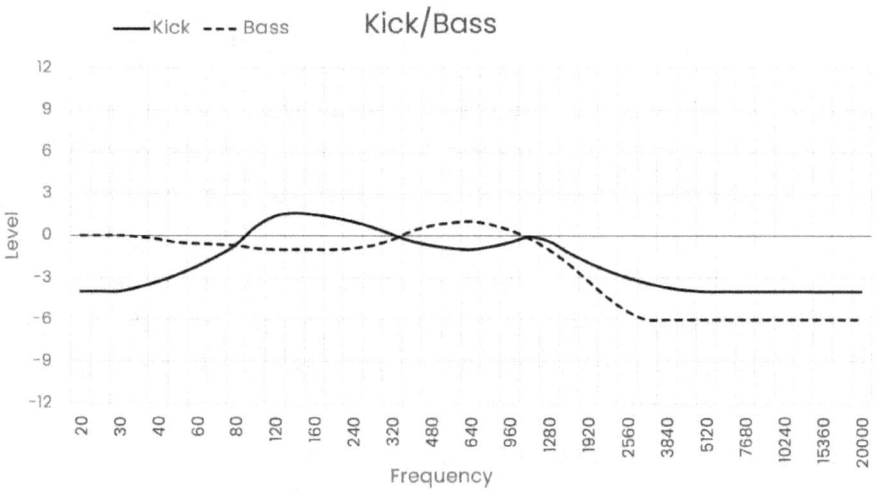

Figure 8.9: *Two EQ curves used to balance a kickdrum with a bassline.*

Next, it was time to analyse the chords. The first issue was the *mud*, which I attenuated using a high-pass filter around 400Hz. With that attenuated, I looked to deal with the *boxiness* of the chords. A resonance around 2kHz caused this, which I attenuated having scanned for the frequency using the technique detailed in Chapter 5.

I then wanted to emphasise the *crunch* generated by a quiet noise oscillator interacting with the sawtooth oscillators of the synthesizer. I scanned for this frequency once again and found it around 4kHz. The best way to emphasise it whilst reducing some of the top end *sparkle* was to use a high shelf filter, tucking it in to create a slight emphasis around 4kHz, whilst dampening some of the *sparkle* of the top end. I show this in Figure 8.10:

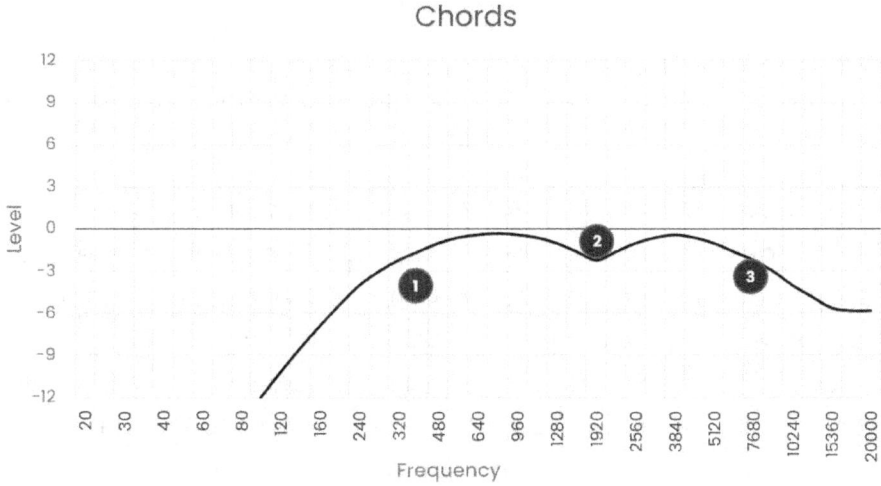

Figure 8.10: An EQ curve used to improve chords.

The next issue was that the ride cymbal didn't *float* in the way I'd have liked it. As detailed in Chapter 6, this can be fixed easily with a high-pass filter around 3kHz and a low-pass filter around 8kHz. In this instance, the ride cymbal lacked *crunch* with the high-pass filter as high as 3kHz, and so I brought its frequency down to around 2kHz. This is detailed in Figure 8.11:

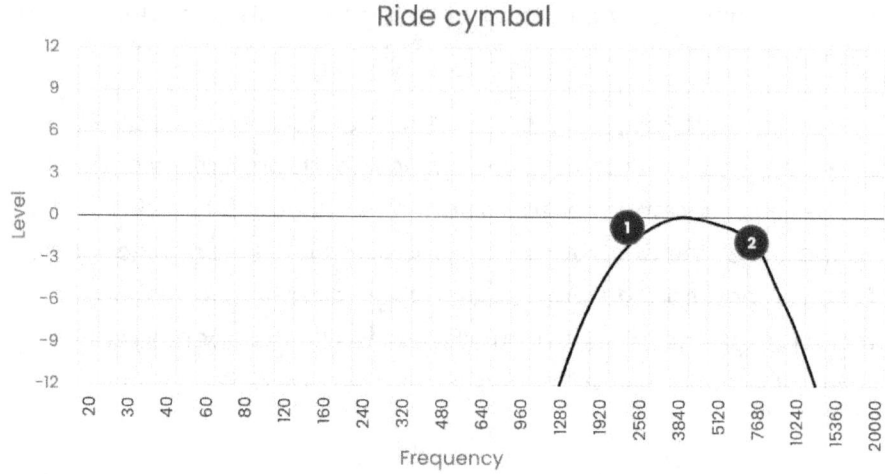

Figure 8.11: An EQ curve used to make a ride cymbal 'float' in the mix.

Finally, I needed to fix the grating resonance in the percussion. I firstly added a high-pass filter around 200Hz to eliminate the noisy junk that took up needless headroom, and I then scanned for the resonance using the Frequency Scanning technique. It popped out strongly around 6kHz, and so I therefore added a bell filter with high Q to attenuate this frequency. Attenuating it too much interfered with the percussion's natural character – I found the best result to be to attenuate it by around -6dB. This is illustrated in Figure 8.12:

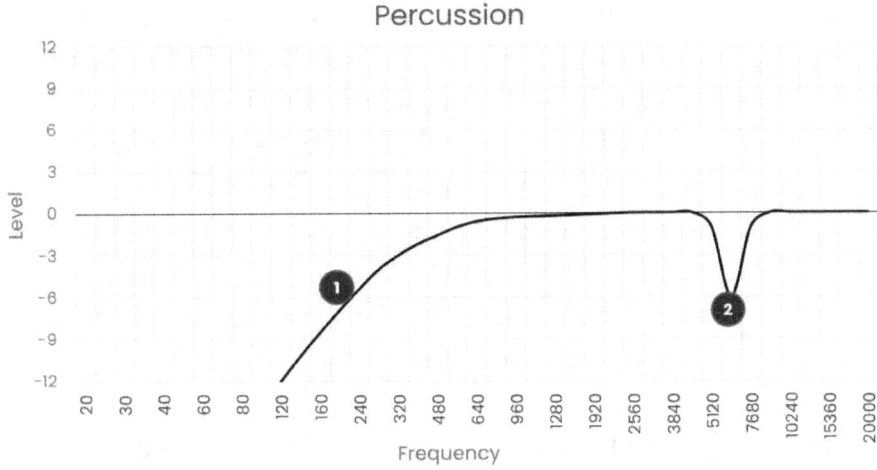

Figure 8.12: An EQ curve used to fix percussion.

With these five parametric EQ curves, the track was transformed from an unbalanced one, with parts of the frequency range that grated, into a pleasant, well-balanced mix.

I'd like to emphasise that this process was relatively easy – a combination of understanding frequency bands, EQing with an aim, and scanning for the correct frequencies yielded effective results. There's no reason you can't do the same, or better, using the knowledge you've gained in this book.

The final chapter is a discussion of cutting-edge EQ techniques that aren't essential to your production workflow but are useful to be aware of. But first, some exercises to show you how far you've come!

Exercises

Follow these instructions:

1. Create a kick and a bass in your DAW. Make sure you use a bass with lots of sub-bass presence. Balance them three different ways using EQ, and see which one you prefer:
    a. The kick is louder in the sub-bass area (below 80Hz), but the bass is louder in the bass area.
    b. The sub-bass is louder in the sub-bass area (below 80Hz), but the kick is louder in the bass area.
    c. The kick is sidechained into the bass so that the bass *ducks* each time the kick plays.

2. Create a synth lead and a synth pad. Enhance each element individually, then balance the two so that they sit together comfortably in the mix.

3. This is the final challenge! If you have a DAW file that you've used EQ in, open it. Remove all instances of EQ and reapply EQ using what you've learned in this book. If you don't have such a DAW file, write a track with these five elements, and EQ them:
    a. A kickdrum
    b. Hi-hats & claps
    c. A shaker or tambourine
    d. A bassline
    e. A lead, or stabs, or a pad

Chapter 9: Advanced EQ Techniques

You should, at this point in the book, feel at least moderately proficient in using EQ. If you don't, I recommend you repeat the exercises in this book. Practice makes perfect!

To finish this book, we will explore EQ techniques that reside on the very cutting edge of music technology. Although you won't use these techniques every day, it's useful to have an awareness of them because you'll never know when you'll need them.

Stereo EQ

The first technique to look at is stereo EQ. This is where independent EQ curves apply to distinct elements of a sound's stereo information. There are two different ways of doing this: one is called Mid/Side EQing and the other one is called Left/Right EQing.

The difference between Left/Right and Mid/Side is that Left/Right treats both your left and right sides independently, whereas Mid/Side splits your stereo track into two signals. The mid signal contains audio information that can be heard in both speakers, whereas the side signal only contains the information that is unique to the left and right speakers. This means that you can treat the centre of your sound and the stereo information of your sound independently.

An excellent example of an EQ that allows you to edit stereo information in this way is Ableton Live's EQ Eight. On the right-hand side of the plugin, you will see a *Mode* parameter. From this, you can select:

- **Stereo**, which allows you to shape the whole mix.
- **M/S**, which allows you to shape the Mid and Side independently of one another.
- **L/R**, which allows you to shape the Left and Right channels independently of one another.

Once you've selected a Mode, you can use the Edit parameter to choose which element of the stereo field to edit. Once you've made your edits, you see that both EQ settings appear in the centre of the plugin interface. This is shown in Figure 9.1 below:

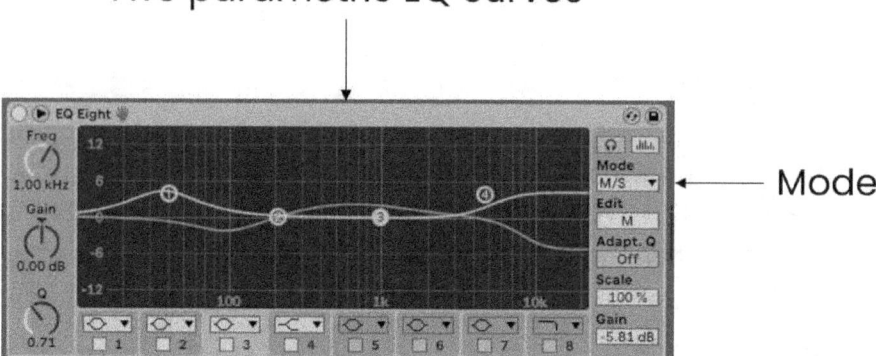

Figure 9.1: *The use of stereo EQ in Ableton Live's EQ Right.*

This type of editing is very useful for sounds where the stereo field is highly important. Examples of this could include brightening the stereo information of a pad or emphasising the delays within a dub techno chord. An example in Figure 9.2 is the use of mid-side EQ to emphasise the stereo information of a Reese bass, whilst keeping the sub-bass area tight.

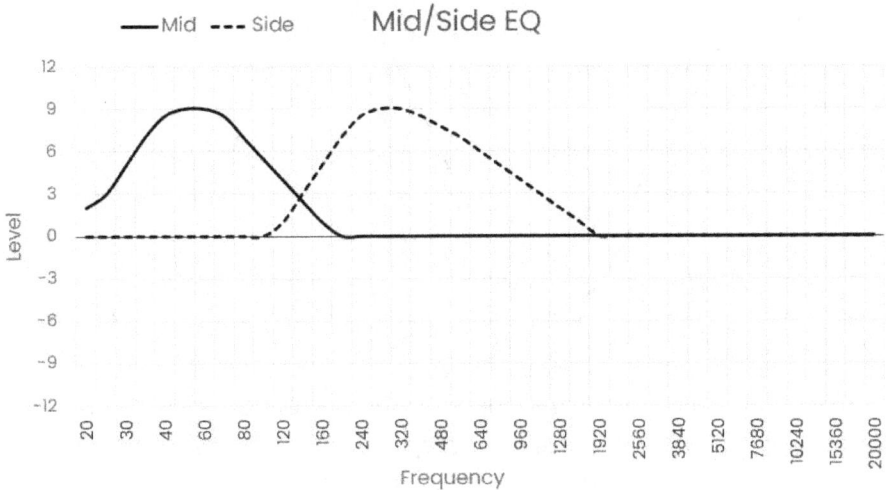

Figure 9.2: An example of two EQ curves used in mid/side EQ.

You should consider stereo EQ on those sounds that occupy the front and centre of your mix - just make sure to check your mix in *Mono* when you've used stereo EQ, to ensure that your changes translate well when the mix is played through a mono system.

Linear Phase EQ

Linear phase EQ is a type of EQ that can only exist in the digital era. Linear phase EQ eliminates phasing issues caused by using EQ. To explain this, let's delve into what audio phase is.

Imagine two symmetrical sine waves playing at the same frequency. When both waves are perfectly aligned, the resultant waveform doubles in amplitude, as shown in Figure 9.3:

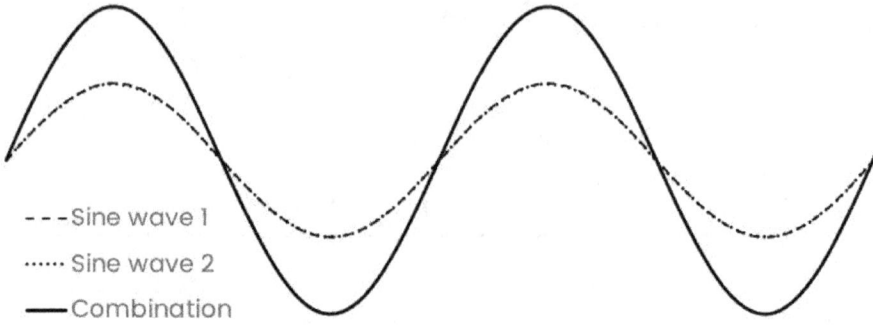

Figure 9.3: Two simultaneous sine waves creating a resultant waveform of double the amplitude of one sine wave.

However, if the starting point of one of these waves is shifted forward or backwards, the resulting waveform changes. For example, if one is moved 90 degrees out of phase, you can see in Figure 9.4 that the resultant waveform has reduced in amplitude:

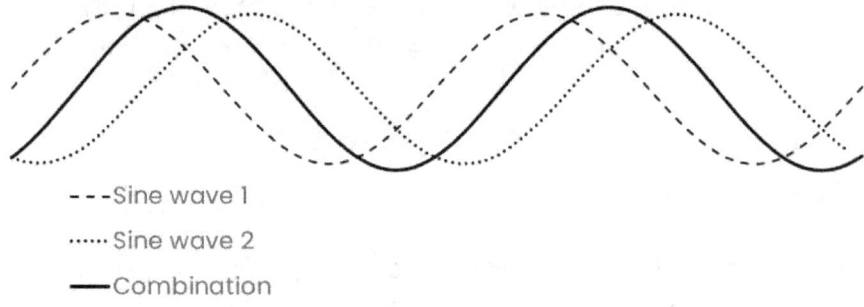

Figure 9.4: Two sine waves 90 degrees out of phase create a resultant waveform the same amplitude as its constituents.

Equally, if one waveform is moved 180 degrees out of phase, you can see in Figure 9.5 that the two wave forms cancel each other out entirely:

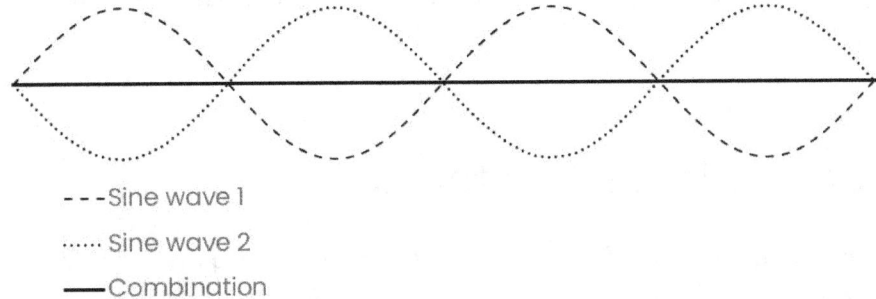

Figure 9.5: Two sine waves 180 degrees out of phase create a resultant waveform of zero amplitude, as they cancel each other out.

EQ plugins, by their very nature, very slightly delay sounds that they're shaping. This is so that they have time to process their changes. This latency can cause phase issues when the EQ'd track is combined with another of similar waveform and frequency.

Linear Phase EQ gives you the option to avoid these phase issues, by analysing the incoming signal and ensuring that EQ changes do not alter the phase of the sound.

However, there are downsides to using Linear Phase EQ. For example, pre-ringing is a is a phenomenon that can sometimes be heard on sharp transients such as drums. This is audible blipping before the transients itself hits. It can sound very displeasing, which affects the overall tonality of the transient. Linear phase EQ can also be quite CPU-heavy.

On this basis, the use of Linear Phase EQ is controversial – some audio engineers swear by it, and others try to avoid it. Whilst it doesn't need to be your go-to EQ plugin, consider its use when EQing a layer that bears strong similarities to another layer in your mix. For example, a recording made on multiple microphones, or a duplicate copy of a track that you're processing in parallel.

Otherwise, there's no urgent or imminent need to use Linear Phase EQ.

Automation: EQ Matching

Groundbreaking plugin companies on now working on ways to automate the process of EQing. There are several ways that they're doing this. The first example is EQ matching. EQ matching is where an algorithm analyses an input channel or audio file of your choice and automatically changes your EQ curve to match the reference that you choose. This can be very useful if you're looking to match the EQ settings of a famous record, for example, or you're looking to recreate your use of EQ on a different track altogether.

Personally, I wouldn't use EQ matching in any of my work – I think it's more important to develop your own sound and style, and so emulating the engineering of others is not important to my process. However, you may wish to consider it if you're trying to recreate the sound of a particular era or artist.

Automation: Dynamic EQ

Another example of automation is the use of Dynamic EQ. This is the shape depends on the amplitude of the input signal. If, for example, you choose to reduce the amplitude of a problem frequency, you can set a range for this reduction. This means that the extent of the reduction in amplitude depends on the input amplitude of your problem frequency. This is illustrated in Figure 9.6:

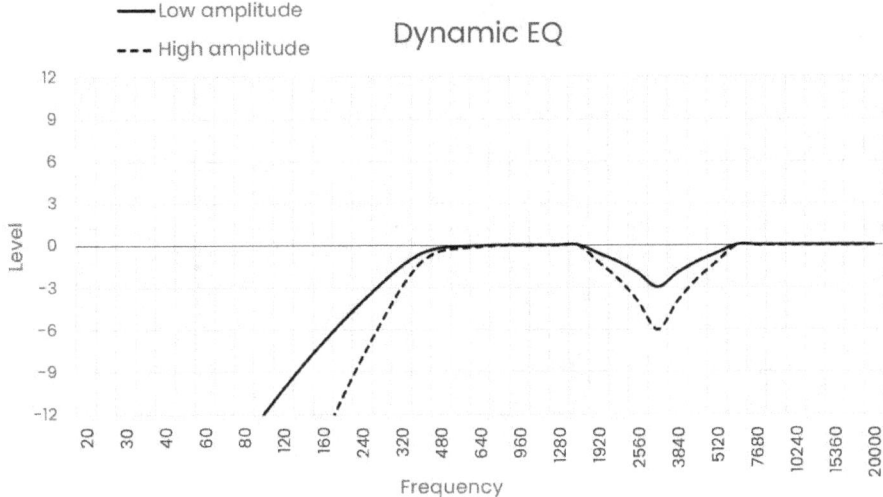

Figure 9.6: An example of EQ that dynamically alters its curve in response to the amplitude of the input signal.

This could be useful when working with instruments that have a wide dynamic range, particularly if this instrument is front and centre of the mix. For example, a solo piano recording may benefit from such a technique.

Automation: Pitch tracking

One issue with precise EQing is that when the notes of the underlying instrument change, so do their frequencies. This can be difficult when you've removed an awkward resonance, only to find that resonance move elsewhere when a different chord is played. Companies are creating EQs to mitigate this, for example Sound Radix's SurferEQ, which dynamically moves the EQ bands in response to the input pitch. This is illustrated in Figure 9.7:

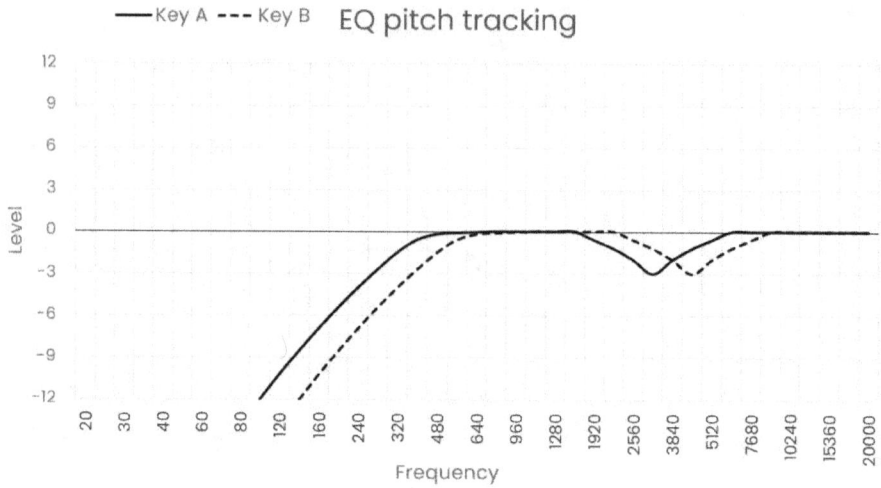

Figure 9.7: An example of a two different EQ curves, depending on the pitch of the input.

This, once again, depends on your needs. I would personally find it to be overkill on day-to-day work, but if you do come across a situation where your EQ needs to move in line with your chords, this is the plugin for you.

Analogue EQ

This book has focused on digital EQ for a reason - it's the type of EQ you will use most often in a computer-based workflow, and it also offers high precision and great visualisation. However, many producers use analogue or analogue-emulating EQ.

The principal reason to use analogue or analogue-emulating EQ is its warmth. Good analogue EQs add pleasing harmonics to your sound, imbuing it with *depth* and *sparkle*. In fact, some analogue EQs can seem to enhance your sound without even being used as an EQ - simply passing your signal through them can add warmth.

Famous examples include the Pultec EQP-1a, the Manley Massive Passive, and the Rupert Neve Designs Portico 5033.

These analogue EQs tend to be of the semi-parametric design, allowing the user to select, boost, and attenuate a few bands.

Analogue EQ, however, does not usually have FFT visualisation. This means that using it correctly requires a fair bit of practice. However, the results in the long term can be worth it.

Analogue-emulating EQ plugins have proliferated recently. The emulations of classic EQs tend to be on the pricey side, although there are some companies, such as Analog Obsession, who provide excellent-quality plugins for a low cost.

Analogue EQ shouldn't necessarily be high on your list of priorities; however, you may find it useful to look into once you've gained a good understanding of using EQ plugins.

Regardless of whether you use analogue EQ in your work, if your mastering engineer uses an analogue workflow, then analogue EQ will be added to your track. Some producers prefer to leave it to the expertise of their mastering engineer to add analogue warmth.

Tilt EQ

Tilt EQ is a particular EQing style available on some plugins. The idea behind tilt is that using the usual filter can interfere with the timbre of a well-balanced sound. For example, attenuating a certain frequency of a piano can make it sound less like a piano.

The answer to this is tilt. Tilt is a filter type that allows you to 'tilt' the frequency range around a pivot, as shown in Figure 9.8:

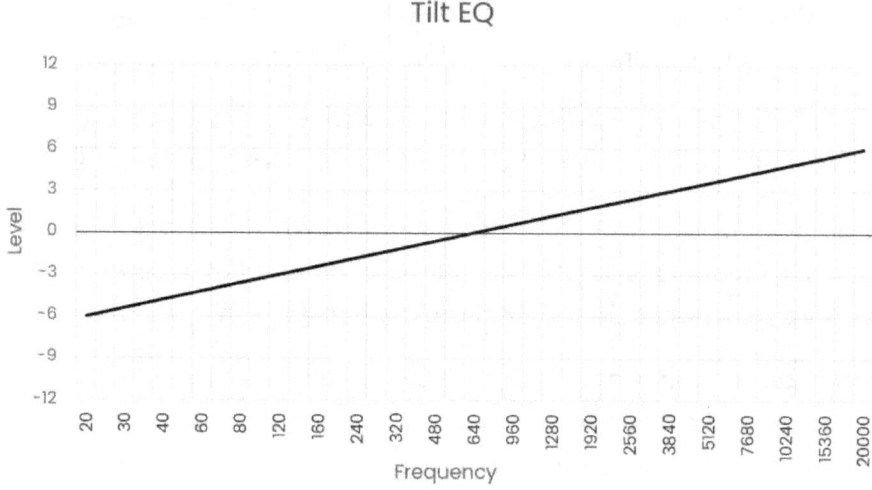

Figure 9.8: An example of a tilt EQ curve.

An example of this could be that you want your piano to shine from around 1.5kHz onwards, so you set your tilt around this threshold. This means that both the top end is enhanced, and the low end is attenuated - but the tonal balance of the instrument is maintained.

Tilt EQ is useful if you're working with instruments that need tweaking in a particular direction, but don't have any glaring issues. Otherwise, if you're looking to troubleshoot, stick with multiband EQ.

Tilt EQ concludes our exploration of the cutting edge of EQ. If you wish to explore this technological forefront in greater detail, the exercises below are a great starting point.

Exercises

Follow these instructions:

1. Research each of the following types of EQ. If you have the function built into your DAW, use it. If you don't, you can download free trials of any plugins that you'd like to try:
    a. Mid/side EQ
    b. Linear phase EQ
    c. Automated EQ (EQ matching)
    d. Automated EQ (Dynamic EQ)
    e. Automated EQ (Pitch tracking)
    f. Analogue EQ
    g. Tilt EQ

Conclusion

Despite the infinite EQ curves possible, getting good results with EQ is relatively easy.

To harness the true potential of EQ, we must approach it with purpose and intent. We shouldn't view it as a tool to tweak and manipulate sound indiscriminately. Instead, let us embrace a mindful approach, treating each EQ adjustment as a deliberate brushstroke on our sonic canvas. With precision and attention to detail, we can shape the audio landscape to meet our specific sonic vision.

As we have seen, the realm of EQ is boundless, offering an abundance of possibilities to sculpt sound according to our desires. The intricate dance between frequencies, the delicate interplay between harmonics and timbres, presents limitless opportunities. While the vast array of EQ curves might initially appear overwhelming, fear not, for achieving exceptional results is well within your grasp.

As you step forward into your next production, remember the power that lies in your hands—the power to shape sound, to evoke emotions, and to create something truly remarkable. Embrace the artistry of EQ, for it is a key that unlocks the boundless potential of your musical expression.

Thank you for reading.

Appendix: Exercise Answers

Chapter 1

1. If you wanted to eliminate frequencies under a set threshold, which filter would you choose?

    a. *Answer:* You would use a **low-pass** filter.

2. If you wanted to add a gentle boost to a frequency in the middle of the frequency range, which filter would you choose?

    Answer: You would use a **bell** filter.

3. If you wanted to attenuate all frequencies above a set threshold, which filter would you choose?

    Answer: You would use a **high-shelf** filter.

4. If your EQing required precision, would you use low Q or high Q?

    Answer: **High Q.**

5. What is "roll-off"?

    Answer: Roll-off defines the **steepness** of the transition from the unfiltered frequencies to the filtered frequencies. A higher roll-off generates a higher degree of steepness.

Chapter 2

1. Where on the frequency spectrum is the sub bass range?

   Answer: The **sub-bass** range is below 80Hz.

2. What is a fundamental frequency?

   Answer: The fundamental frequency, **distinct from the harmonics, is the lowest frequency of the waveform of a musical note**. For example, if you play middle C on a keyboard (256Hz), the fundamental frequency will be at 256Hz.

3. What frequency is the third harmonic of a note playing at 800Hz?

   Answer: 800Hz × 3 = **1,600Hz** (usually shortened to 1.6kHz).

4. In which part of the frequency spectrum would you find *sparkle*?

   Answer: The sparkle is found **above 7kHz**.

Chapter 4

1. What type of EQ is most commonly found on DJ mixers?

   Answer: Graphic EQ is most commonly found on DJ mixers.

2. What does the Frequency parameter do on semi-parametric EQ?

   Answer: The Frequency parameter allows you to select the crossover frequency between bands.

3. What's the difference between parametric EQ and semi-parametric EQ?

   Answer: Whereas semi parametric EQ has a fixed number of frequency bands, parametric EQ offers complete flexibility as to the number of filters in use, the type of filters used, each filter's frequency, and each filter's Q value.

Chapter 6

1. Why is using an EQ preset a bad idea?

   Answer: The designers of EQ presets **can't hear** the context of your mix, can't hear the exact timbre of the instrument that you're using, and they don't know your aims. You're better off learning about EQ and using your own knowledge.

2. Why should you normally subtract, instead of adding frequencies?

   Answer: Adding frequencies takes up **headroom**, giving you less room to manoeuvre in your mix.

3. Why shouldn't you simply EQ every track in your mix?

    Answer: There are three main reasons to use EQ: **balance, remove** frequencies you don't want, and **enhance** frequencies you do want. If a sound doesn't need any of these treatments, using EQ will worsen your sound, and add an unnecessary layer of complexity to your mix.

www.ingramcontent.com/pod-product-compliance
Lightning Source LLC
Chambersburg PA
CBHW071003080526
44587CB00015B/2320